D1340252

LONDON AFTER THE BOMB

This book was written by five university research scientists (the LATB Study Group) who were brought together by their common concern about nuclear arms, and by the belief that on issues such as these, scientists have a special responsibility to society. Owen Greene, Dr Barry Rubin, Neil Turok, and Dr Philip Webber (who acted as co-ordinator) are at Imperial College, University of London; Dr Graeme Wilkinson is at the University of Reading.

LONDON
AFTER
THE
BOMB

WHAT A NUCLEAR ATTACK
REALLY MEANS

Owen Greene
Barry Rubin
Neil Turok
Philip Webber
Graeme Wilkinson

Oxford   New York

OXFORD UNIVERSITY PRESS

1982

Oxford University Press, Walton Street, Oxford OX2 6DP

London Glasgow New York Toronto
Delhi Bombay Calcutta Madras Karachi
Kuala Lumpur Singapore Hong Kong Tokyo
Nairobi Dar es Salaam Cape Town
Melbourne Auckland
and associates in
Beirut Berlin Ibadan Mexico City Nicosia

British Library Cataloguing in Publication Data

London after the bomb: what a nuclear attack
really means.—(Oxford paperbacks)
1. Atomic warfare 2. London (England)
—Bombardment
I. Greene, Owen
355'.0217 UF767
ISBN 0–19–285123–3

Printed in Great Britain by
Cox & Wyman Ltd
Reading, Berks

Acknowledgements

We want to thank all the many people who helped in the writing and the preparation of this book for press. In particular we want to thank Dr Trevor Hall, Dr David Caplin, June Power, Jane Davis, Suzanne Cheston, Steve Abbott, Hugh Gordon, and Professor Tom Kibble for their help and encouragement, and P. Steadman, N. Barford, Dr M. Barnett, Professor F. Pirani, Professor M. Wilkins, and Professor J. Rotblat for reading and commenting on the text. We thank all the staff of Oxford University Press and particularly Nicola Bion, Henry Hardy, and Susan le Roux for their hard work and valuable suggestions. We also thank the Greater London Council for their co-operation. Finally, we acknowledge the support of Scientists Against Nuclear Arms (SANA), the organisation which brought us together.

Contents

List of Illustrations

Figure 13 is redrawn from *Protect and Survive* by kind permission of the Controller of Her Majesty's Stationery Office.

Illustrations by Illustra Design

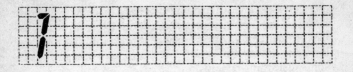

Introduction

In an all-out nuclear war, more destructive power than in all of World War Two would be unleashed every second for the long afternoon it would take for all the missiles and bombs to fall. A world war every second – more people killed in the first few hours than [in] all the wars of history put together. The survivors, if any, would live in despair amid the poisoned ruins of a civilization that had committed suicide ...

President Jimmy Carter in his Farewell Address to the Nation,
14 January 1981

This is a vision of the ultimate catastrophe for all mankind. But is this vision realistic? Would it really be the end, or would a war like this be survivable? In Britain the idea of effective civil defence against nuclear war has recently been revived and is now the subject of intense debate.

In view of this controversy and in the light of recent developments which increase the risk of nuclear war, we decided to carry out an independent study to see what nuclear war would really mean. We have used the most reliable scientific information available to find out what would be most likely to happen if Britain were ever to be attacked. We have taken London as our main example, but broadly speaking our findings relate to any city in Britain. By focusing on a particular area, a very clear picture emerges of how the lives of ordinary people would be affected.

Throughout this book the effects of nuclear attack are described not only in numbers but also in terms of what a person would be likely to see and feel. Wherever possible, our findings and their implications are compared with Home Office information and advice freely available in Government publications, as well as with information from Home Office internal circulars. Our research has led us to some disturbing conclusions.

☐ The growing risk of nuclear war

A nuclear war might start by accident at any time. The computers required to detect attack and to control the large numbers of highly sophisticated weapons-systems repeatedly fail. We have already survived many false 'red alerts', but one day the error may be found too late. The increased accuracy of the newer missiles has made missile silos themselves vulnerable. They are in danger of being destroyed in a surprise attack. This may soon lead to the adoption of a 'launch on warning' policy which would increase the chances of an accidental start to a nuclear war.

Over the last decade, military strategists have increasingly envisaged fighting a 'limited nuclear war' in Europe. This would involve the early use of smaller, 'battlefield', nuclear weapons after the outbreak of a conventional war. Many military authorities believe that this would rapidly escalate into an all-out nuclear war.

It is also possible that a nuclear war might start elsewhere in the world. The acquisition of nuclear weapons by regimes in politically unstable regions in which both superpowers are involved, such as the Middle East, makes this all the more likely.

☐ The civil defence controversy

Recently, the British Government has promoted the idea of civil defence against nuclear attack on Britain. In contrast, to quote Lord Zuckerman, Chief Scientific Advisor to the Ministry of Defence for six years:

As the British Government's White Paper on Defence put it as long ago as 1957,[1] there are no means of protecting the population against the consequences of a nuclear attack. There are none today, when the scale of attack that could be envisaged is at least a hundred times greater than it was twenty years ago.[2]

Yet today quite a different message is presented in recent Home Office publications such as *Protect and Survive, Domestic Nuclear Shelters*, and *Civil Defence – why we need it*. These publications present simple civil defence measures as both practical and effective. There has been no official justification for this change in policy.

□ This book

Debate about nuclear war is, understandably, often passionate and heated, with vested interest and political preconceptions often more to the fore than objective examination of the arguments. This makes it especially important for those who want their contribution to the debate to be responsible and reliable to proceed with caution, and above all with respect for the available evidence. This has been our firm commitment in writing this book. Nevertheless, it is only natural that we have strong feelings about the conclusions we reached, and although we have tried to let the facts speak for themselves we have not attempted the rather artificial exercise of concealing our views altogether. Some of the criticisms to which the book may be subjected are worth clearing up at the outset.

First, because there has never been a large-scale nuclear attack on any country, a study of the consequences must be based on extrapolations from previous evidence and must have some degree of uncertainty. This is not to say that such a study cannot be well founded – and indeed we believe that our conclusions are as soundly based as the available data permit.

Secondly, the book was not written solely in support of

any particular political viewpoint. Naturally enough we have our own political views, and these have been informed by the findings reported in this book. Also, naturally, we believe that these views are reasonable and defensible. But our specific conclusions about civil defence are of immediate and vital importance to everyone, whatever his or her political outlook. It would be sad folly to turn a blind eye to these conclusions by the irrelevant device of branding them with a political label. Nobody can evade the questions that our findings raise.

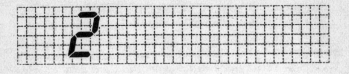

The
Nuclear
Bomb

In a nuclear explosion the powerful forces which bind together the structures of atoms are suddenly released. There are two ways in which this can be done, known as 'fission' and 'fusion'. In the fission or atomic bomb (A-bomb) such as destroyed Hiroshima, energy is released by splitting the nucleus of very heavy atoms such as uranium or plutonium. In the fusion or thermonuclear bomb (H-bomb) the reverse process occurs and light atoms such as tritium or deuterium combine to form helium. In both the fission and fusion reactions immense power is released as heat, light, and radiation. The power of the fission bomb is limited by the amount of heavy atomic material that can be brought together to react. In the fusion bomb, a fission explosion is used to trigger the fusion reaction which is potentially much more destructive.

Because of the highly destructive nature of nuclear weapons, the effects that they produce are usually related to an equivalent explosive power in *thousands or millions of tons* of the high explosive TNT. The equivalent of one thousand tons is called a kiloton (kT) and the equivalent of one million tons a megaton (MT).

Despite the fact that their explosive power is measured in equivalent amounts of TNT, nuclear weapons are

Nuclear radiation

There are four major sorts of nuclear radiation: very energetic X-rays called gamma radiation; and beams of neutrons, helium nuclei, and electrons, called neutron, alpha, and beta radiation. Radiation is normally given off only by the so-called radioactive elements such as uranium or radium. In the nuclear bomb this radiation is produced in the fission and fusion reactions. Intense neutron radiation from a nuclear bomb can make ordinary materials radioactive, so that they then give off radiation themselves. (See Figure 1)

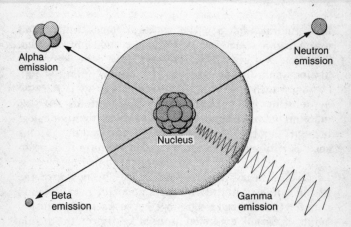

Fig. 1 Release of radiation from the nucleus of a radioactive atom

fundamentally different from 'conventional' non-nuclear weapons in three important ways:

● Intense nuclear radiation is given off during the fission or fusion reaction.
● A brilliantly hot fire-ball is produced which can severely burn or blind people many miles away from the explosion (even before the blast reaches them).

● Radioactive materials are produced as a by-product of
  the fission reaction, which can be a serious health hazard
  long after the bomb has exploded. This hazard can also
  be made worse by adding more fissionable material to
  make a so-called 'dirty' bomb producing even more
  radioactivity.

In a nuclear war, land targets can be attacked by
exploding bombs either at several thousand feet above the
ground (an air-burst) or on the ground (a ground-burst) (see
Figure 2). The air-burst causes the most blast and fire
damage because it avoids the shielding effect of the ground.
The ground-burst produces a crater and so does most
damage close to its target. Powerful updraughts of hot air
are produced by the fire-ball. The radioactive remains of the
bomb, and dust and soil particles made radioactive by
intense nuclear radiation, are carried high into the air.
These radioactive particles are called fall-out: they fall back
to the ground over periods ranging from minutes for the
largest to many years for the smallest.

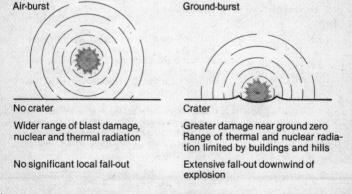

Air-burst

No crater

Wider range of blast damage,
nuclear and thermal radiation

No significant local fall-out

Ground-burst

Crater

Greater damage near ground zero
Range of thermal and nuclear radiation limited by buildings and hills

Extensive fall-out downwind of
explosion

Fig. 2 Differences between an air-burst and a ground-burst

☐ The effects of a single one-megaton nuclear bomb

To illustrate the destructive power of a nuclear bomb, imagine that you are cocooned inside a totally protective transparent shell positioned about three and a half miles from the point on the ground directly beneath the explosion (known as 'ground zero'), watching the air-burst of a one-megaton bomb at an altitude of 6,000 feet.

Immediately after the detonation a short flash of light is emitted of an intensity sufficient to blind anyone looking towards it. Within three seconds an intensely hot fire-ball some 6,000 feet across is formed. You see the clothes of people in the open or inside near windows catch fire from the heat of the fire-ball and their exposed skin charred with third degree burns. Curtains and any other exposed inflammable materials catch fire. Within 12 seconds a blast wave travelling slightly faster than the speed of sound reaches you, accompanied by winds of up to 200 m.p.h.

Medical description of burns

Level of flash-burns (degree)	Medical effect
Third	Full thickness of skin and some underlying tissue killed. Skin is red or charred. Severe pain from edges of burns. Burns over 2 inches in diameter will heal only after extended specialised treatment including skin grafting. Untreated victim may die of shock if over 20% of the body is affected.
Second	Upper and intermediate layers of skin killed. Blisters and swelling develop, accompanied by persistent pain. Extensive burns require specialised treatment in sterile conditions. Healing over several weeks, leaving scarring.
First	Mildest form of burns. Immediate pain followed by redness of affected area. Will heal without scar formation.

---

already laden with large pieces of debris. For comparison, the wind speeds in a naturally occurring hurricane rarely exceed 120 m.p.h. Ordinary brick-built or timber-framed houses are not designed to withstand such forces. You see them reduced to rubble, burying the people inside and blocking the streets. Cars are tossed about like toys, and lamp standards and telegraph poles blown to the ground. Anyone standing in the open is lifted bodily and blown over long distances (this is rather drily known as translation) and may collide at high speed with any object left standing. You see people crushed or trapped inside their houses under falling masonry, or severely injured by flying bricks, glass, and other debris. Much further out, in the open, as far as eight miles from the explosion, you could still be blinded by the flash and in average visibility receive second degree burns. At this distance the blast wave arrives 30 seconds after the explosion and smashes windows, blows in doors, and damages roofs. Cuts from flying glass are the most common blast injury.

Figure 3 shows an impression of the effects of a one-megaton air-burst exploded at 6,000 feet over Trafalgar Square in London. Such a bomb, which is not exceptionally large by current standards, would destroy an area of London about 10 miles across, and cause widespread damage over a much larger area (see Table 1 for the extent of blast and fire damage). A one-megaton ground-burst, by contrast with an air-burst, would cause an enormous crater some 1,300 feet across and 250 feet deep. To give an idea of size, this crater is large enough to accommodate ten Wembley Stadiums. A vast quantity of soil would be made radioactive and sucked up into a mushroom-shaped cloud about 10 miles across. This material would come down later as fall-out.

□ Casualties

The three main effects of a nuclear explosion which kill and injure people are blast, heat, and radiation. For air-bursts in

2 seconds after detonation

Kew Gardens Greenhouse · Parliament Hill · Albert Hall · Nelson's Column · St. Paul's · Tower Bridge · Greenwich Observatory · Woolwich Docks

Blast wave
Initial radiation
Fire-ball

11 seconds after detonation

Reflected blast wave
Blast wave
Winds of 180 m.p.h.
6 p.s.i.

p.s.i. = pounds per square inch

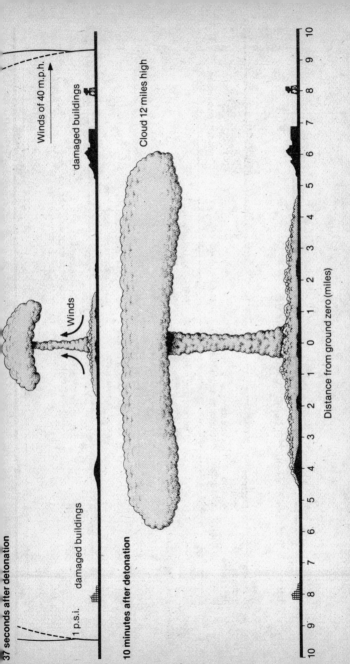

37 seconds after detonation

Winds of 40 m.p.h.

damaged buildings

1 p.s.i.

damaged buildings

Winds

10 minutes after detonation

Cloud 12 miles high

Distance from ground zero (miles)

10 9 8 7 6 5 4 3 2 1 0 1 2 3 4 5 6 7 8 9 10

Fig. 3 Effects of blast of a 1 MT nuclear bomb exploded at 6,000 ft over Trafalgar Square

Table 1 Effects of a 1 MT nuclear bomb exploded at 6000 ft

Blast pressure (pounds per square inch)	Zone	Distance from ground zero (miles)	Fire damage (visibility about 12 miles)	Blast damage	Area (square miles)	Typical city population
			Steel surfaces melt, concrete surfaces explode, glass windows melt	Bridges and multi-storey concrete buildings destroyed. Cars and lorries blown long distances	9	225,000
	A	1.7				
			Aluminium window-frames melt, car metal melts	Multi-storey concrete buildings destroyed or near to collapse	11	275,000
12		2.5				
	B		Severe fire zone. Wood, roofing-felt burst into flames	Unreinforced brick or timber-frame houses destroyed. Multi-storey concrete buildings severely damaged	31	775,000
5		4				

5

— 4

— C 5.5

Upholstery, canvas, clothing burst into flames. Painted surfaces explode

Unreinforced brick or timber-frame houses damaged beyond repair. Telephone lines blown down

45

1,125,000

Severe 3rd degree burns, grass and shrubs catch fire

Timber-frame houses damaged beyond repair. Brick houses damaged but repairable

59

1,475,000

2

— 7

Severe 2nd degree burns. People flash-blinded by reflected light

Trees blown down. Brick and timber-frame houses damaged but repairable

101

2,525,000

— D 9

1st degree burns

Windows and doors blown in. Interior partitions cracked

60

1,500,000

1

— 10

the one-megaton range and for normal city targets it is blast and fire which kill or injure the largest number of people. In the case of a ground-burst many more casualties may result from radiation days or weeks after the explosion. These later casualties may eventually exceed those from all other causes. This is because fall-out can cover much larger areas than those damaged by blast or fire.

Blast

Most immediate casualties are a result of blast. People are either hurled into objects, struck violently by debris, or crushed under collapsing buildings. Intense blast-pressure can also kill or injure directly by rupturing the lungs, eardrums, or other internal organs. Casualties expected in areas experiencing various blast pressure levels have been estimated by many authorities. The most reliable information is based upon the Japanese Second World War casualties in Hiroshima and Nagasaki and data from above-ground nuclear bomb tests conducted before the partial Nuclear Test Ban Treaty of October 1963. There is substantial agreement between the Japanese[3] and American data (the Office of Technology Assessment[4] and the US Department of Defense and Department of Energy[5]), which all give extensive references to other studies. These sources disagree sharply with the UK Home Office expected casualty levels as given in *Domestic Nuclear Shelters: Technical Guidance.* US authorities in fact expect two and a half times more fatal blast casualties than the Home Office (calculated for a one-megaton ground-burst and uniform population density). The two main reasons for this are:

● The Home Office assumes that high blast pressures are confined to smaller areas than those given by the American sources (see Table 2, rings a and b).
● For a given level of blast the Home Office expects a smaller proportion of people to be killed or injured (see Table 2, rings b and c).

Table 2 Comparison of expected blast casualties from a 1 MT ground-burst

Home Office designation	Blast pressure (pounds per square inch)	Extent of blast (miles)		Deaths and injuries	
		Home Office	US Dept of Defense and OTA	Home Office	OTA†
a ring	11 p.s.i. and over	up to 1½	up to 2	High probability of death or serious injury	98% deaths
b ring	6 to 11 p.s.i.	1½ to 2¼	2 to 2½	About 10% killed; 35% trapped; others injured	50% killed 40% injured
c ring	1.5 to 6 p.s.i.	2¼ to 5½	2½ to 6	About 25% trapped or seriously injured at inner edge of ring (2¼ miles)	5% killed 45% injured
d ring	0.75 to 1.5 p.s.i.	6* to 9	6 to 9	No deaths; few injuries expected	No deaths 25% injured

* This figure is as in *Domestic Nuclear Shelters: Technical Guidance* and should read 5½.
† These OTA figures apply to the blast Zones A, B, C, and D defined overleaf.

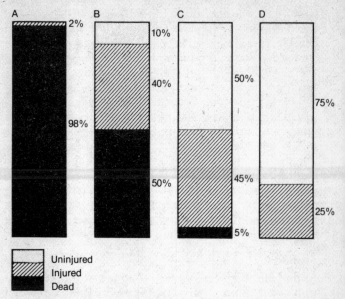

Fig. 4 Percentage blast casualties

The numbers of casualties from Hiroshima,[3] once scaled
up for a one-megaton ground-burst, agree very well with the
US data. As the Home Office provides no details of how
their estimates were obtained and since all other sources of
information contradict their findings, we regard the Home
Office figures as under-estimates. In our view, the Office of
Technology Assessment (OTA) estimates are more realistic
and hence form the basis of calculations in this study. We
have calculated casualties from blast by taking proportions
of the numbers of people in Zones A,B,C, and D, defined by
blast-pressure levels of over 12, 12–5, 5–2, and 2–1 pounds
per square inch respectively (see Figure 4).

Burns and fire

People in the open or near windows can receive serious or

fatal burns. The heat of the fire-ball also starts widespread fires: in houses, curtains and furniture are set alight. Outside, fires are started in petrol stations, gas works, or by burst gas mains. Individual fires may join together to form one huge fire – a *fire-storm* or a *conflagration*. In a fire-storm, such as those experienced in Dresden, Hamburg, and Hiroshima in the Second World War, hurricane-force winds are sucked in by the fire. Temperatures of 1,000 °C or more can be reached, sufficient to melt glass and some metals. People are incinerated or suffocated. In a conflagration the fires spread outwards until there is nothing left to burn, killing those trapped in houses or too badly injured to escape. Even smouldering fires can cause death by reducing the amount of oxygen in the air and producing carbon monoxide or other toxic gases: a shelter would not necessarily afford any protection in these circumstances.

Radiation

As the bomb explodes, intense radiation consisting primarily of neutrons and gamma rays is emitted. Up to a mile and a half away an unprotected person receives a lethal dose of radiation. People this close to the explosion, however, are killed anyway by blast and heat.

The most important longer-term effect for ground-bursts or near-surface bursts is fall-out. Over a period of a few hours after detonation, unprotected people as far as 50–100 miles downwind of the explosion may receive a deadly dose of radiation from fall-out.

Fall-out particles are spread by the wind and come down from the atmosphere in a very unpredictable way because of local variations in land relief, wind, clouds, and rain. So the spread of fall-out from a bomb cannot be predicted accurately. These variations were seen in the fall-out pattern of a small test nuclear explosion detonated at the Nevada Test Site on 28 May 1957 – the 'Boltzmann Shot'. 'Hot spots' of radiation were formed, 20 square miles in area and 10 times more radioactive than their surroundings (see Figure 5a).

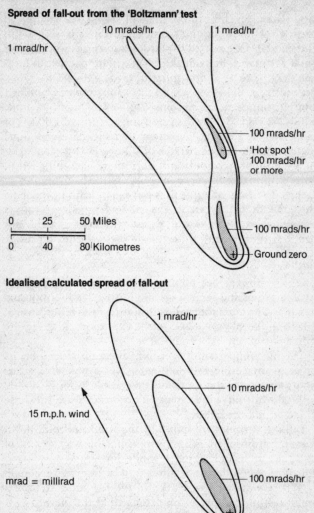

Spread of fall-out from the 'Boltzmann' test

10 mrads/hr

1 mrad/hr

1 mrad/hr

100 mrads/hr

'Hot spot'
100 mrads/hr
or more

100 mrads/hr

Ground zero

0   25   50 Miles

0   40   80 Kilometres

Idealised calculated spread of fall-out

1 mrad/hr

10 mrads/hr

15 m.p.h. wind

mrad = millirad

100 mrads/hr

Fig. 5 Comparison of actual and calculated fall-out distribution from a small test explosion (redrawn from Glasstone and Dolan[5])

For the purposes of making rough estimates, planners usually assume that the wind speed is a steady 15 m.p.h. without direction changes. The radiation contours arising from these calculations form an idealised cigar shape (see Figure 5b) which is very unlikely to be found in reality. The value of such calculations, however, is that they give a rough idea of the areas over which radiation may be expected.

The effect of radiation on the body is to damage or destroy the internal structure of cells.[6] In particular, red and white blood-cell and sperm production is impaired and the stomach and intestine linings degenerate. Radiation at all levels does some damage (see Table 3) but symptoms such as nausea, vomiting, diarrhoea, and hair loss become

---

Radiation dose units

● The most common unit of radiation dose is the *rad*, which is used to describe the absorption of energy in a given material from any form of radiation. One rad is defined as the energy transfer of 100 ergs per gram into the material (a 100–watt light bulb emits 1,000 million ergs per second): this is a relatively small amount of energy, but it can enter directly into cells where it can do substantial damage. The level of biological damage differs, depending upon the type of radiation giving the dose. The factor used to measure this (relative to the effect of X-rays) is known as the Quality Factor (QF). The approximate values of QF for the four different types of nuclear radiation are:

Beta and gamma radiation	QF= 1
Neutrons	QF=10
Alpha particles	QF=20

This gives another unit of radiation dose (the *rem*) which is calculated by multiplying the dose in rads by the relevant Quality Factor. This unit more accurately represents the degree of biological damage caused by the radiation exposure. For beta and gamma radiation, and X-rays, one rem is equal to one rad. We have used rads throughout since the range of alpha particle emission is very short and neutrons are not given off by fall-out.

Table 3 Medical effects of radiation

Dose (rads)	Symptoms	Deaths (average)
0–100	Men become temporarily sterile in 20–50 rads range	0
100–200	Nausea and vomiting within 3–6 hours of receiving dose and lasting less than 1 day, followed by no symptoms for 2 weeks. Recurrence of symptoms for another 4 weeks. Number of white blood cells reduced	0
200–600	Nausea and vomiting lasting 1–2 days. No symptoms for 1–4 weeks followed by a recurrence of symptoms for up to 8 weeks. Diarrhoea, severe reduction of white blood cells, blood blisters on skin, bleeding, infection. Loss of hair above 300 rads	0–98% in 2–12 weeks from internal bleeding or infection
600–1,000	Nausea and vomiting starting within ½ hour of receiving dose of radiation and lasting 2 days. No symptoms for 5–10 days then same symptoms as for 200–600 rads for 1–4 weeks	98–100% from internal bleeding or infection
1,000–5,000	Nausea and vomiting starting within ½ hour of receiving dose and lasting less than a day. No symptoms for about 7 days, then diarrhoea, fever, disturbed salt balance in blood for 2–14 days	100% within 14 days from collapse of circulation
more than 5,000	Nausea and vomiting immediately followed by convulsions, loss of control of movement and lethargy	100% in 48 hours from failure of breathing or brain damage

Note: Effects apply only for a normal population of adults receiving total radiation doses over short periods of time, and may vary very widely in the 100–600 rad range.

increasingly common as dose levels rise above 100 rads. The body's resistance to infection is lowered by damage to the skin and mucous membranes, and by reduced white blood-cell and antibody production. Bacteria, however, display a resistance to radiation some thousand to a million times greater than human cells: one strain of bacteria has even been found growing in the water cooler of a nuclear reactor. As a result of the damage caused to the body's defences and the resistance of bacteria to radiation, infection becomes a very serious problem. Treatment with antibiotics further complicates the situation since the presence of these drugs slows down the repair of radiation-damaged cells.

In the 200–600 rad range and above there will be an increasing number of deaths. For every 100 healthy adults exposed over a day or two to a dose of 400 rads, and without intensive hospital care, about 50 survive. At a dose of 600 rads hardly anyone will survive.[7] Babies and children, the injured, the sick, and the elderly are much more vulnerable to radiation sickness. Treatment of patients who have received non-fatal doses of radiation requires rest, good nutrition, and maintenance of body fluids. At doses of 300 rads or more, intensive hospital care is needed as well as blood transfusions or bone marrow transplants.

At doses below 100 rads people are unlikely to die as a direct result of radiation but may still suffer some of the symptoms of radiation sickness. They or their descendants may suffer from genetic damage or die later from radiation-induced cancers.

After the blast and fire have done their damage, the survivors then face the danger of radiation from fall-out. Fall-out dust settles on the ground, on roofs, and on other surfaces, and may enter houses through any openings. The radiation given off cannot be detected by any of the human senses. People without radiation detectors cannot know how much radiation they are receiving or whether they are in danger. They may also breathe in or swallow radioactive dust without knowing it.

The radiation dose that one receives is reduced by distance from the source of radiation and by any intervening materials. The amount by which a house or shelter reduces the radiation is called the 'Protection Factor'(PF). The actual dose received from fall-out is given by the level of radiation outside divided by the protection factor of any shelter. For example, if the dose rate outside is 1,000 rads per hour and the shelter has a protection factor of 5, anyone sheltering inside will receive a dose of 200 rads per hour. This factor is obviously critical in determining how many radiation casualties there are. But certainly the areas which can be covered by fall-out from a ground-burst are much

Nagasaki

● Japanese experiences after the attacks on Hiroshima and Nagasaki in the Second World War show that radiation affects different individuals at different rates; some people died very quickly from radiation sickness and others, even from the same family, died much more slowly. A doctor from Nagasaki recalls the following experience:

'within seven to ten days after the A-bomb explosion, people began to die in swift succession. They died of burns that covered their bodies and of acute atomic disease [radiation sickness]. Innumerable people who had been burnt turned a mulberry colour, like worms, and died. It was terrible, but death coming so suddenly, so abruptly, left me little time to brood. Even so, the ensuing forty days caused me much sorrow and grief. For the disease that infected the people – whether the atomic disease or some purulent condition associated with it – destroyed them little by little. . . .

Even where two people who had been in the same place when the A-bomb exploded, the same symptoms did not necessarily develop in each of them at the same time, or in the same way. It seemed that the younger members of each family had the least resistance to the disease and died the sooner. On the other hand, should they manage to get over the worst, the sooner they sometimes got better.

The day after one young girl died, her elder sister began to lose her hair. Crying over the younger sister, she said: 'I now have all the same symptoms as she had. I'll surely die.'

Her father, suffering from similar symptoms, looked down at his daughter sadly, already resigned to die – a sequence of despair that lasted forty days.'[8]

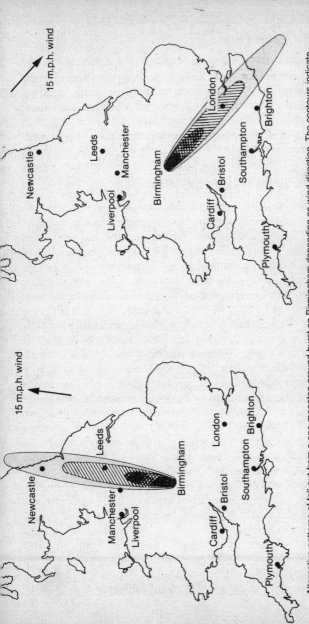

Alternative patterns of fall-out from a one-megaton ground-burst on Birmingham depending on wind direction. The contours indicate seven-day accumulated doses of 3,000, 400, 100, 30 rads to unprotected people. A dose of 400 rads will kill about half those exposed to it.

Fig. 6 Fall-out plumes from a 1 MT ground-burst

larger than those damaged by blast or fire. Because of the large numbers of people likely to be in areas of high fall-out (see Figure 6), the number of deaths caused by radiation would be higher than those from blast and fire combined. Also the lingering and unpleasant nature of radiation sickness causes extensive human suffering. People may take over two months to die.

□ The Electro-Magnetic Pulse

Another effect of the nuclear bomb, which does not directly affect buildings or people, is known as the Electro-Magnetic Pulse (EMP).[9] This is an extremely intense but very short burst of radio waves which can knock out electrical networks and communications systems over a considerable distance. The pulse from just one very high-altitude explosion can be received over an area hundreds of miles in radius. For example, in 1962 a test explosion over Johnston Island in the Pacific Ocean put out the street lights on the island of Oahu 800 miles away.[5] This violent burst of radio energy can cause damaging surges of current in almost all forms of electrical and electronic equipment. These surges may be so strong that measures designed to protect against similar effects produced by lightning are inadequate against nuclear EMP. The circuits worst affected are those with any sensitive components, as found in computers; those which pick up and amplify radio signals, as in radios, televisions, and radar sets; and those attached to long lengths of cable such as telephones and the electricity power grid. Such damage could be inflicted throughout the whole of Northern Europe by just one nuclear bomb exploded at an altitude of 100 miles. Three explosions could affect all of North America or Russia.

Protection against the EMP is known as 'hardening' and takes the form of shielding sensitive circuits by placing them inside conducting boxes (Faraday cages), or by using less sensitive components (radio valves or optical fibre links). Civilian equipment is of course not EMP-hardened. A high-altitude nuclear explosion would be very likely to damage all television sets and many radio receivers. Electricity supplies would also be affected. As a result of this, after a nuclear attack, the Government or the Regional Controllers (see page 83) might be unable to communicate with survivors by radio or by television.

☐ Summary

- A single one-megaton nuclear bomb can destroy by blast and fire an area 10 miles across.

- People can be killed by blast, heat, or intense nuclear radiation from the initial explosion, by fires, or by the radiation dose accumulated from radioactive fall-out dust over the next few weeks.

- The spread of radioactive fall-out is unpredictable but is likely to kill more people than the combined effects of blast and fire.

- Radiation damages cells in the body, reduces the ability to fight infection, and may lead to a lingering death. It also causes genetic damage and cancers, which become apparent only in the long term.

- The Electro-Magnetic Pulse caused by a high-altitude nuclear explosion can damage electronic circuits over a very wide area. Therefore Government or Regional Controllers might be unable to communicate with survivors by radio or television after the attack.

- Home Office blast casualty estimates are much too low. US estimates are over twice as high.

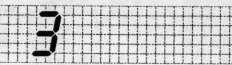

The Consequences of a Nuclear Attack on London

☐ Operation Square Leg

In September 1980 various Government departments conducted an exercise, code-named Operation Square Leg, as
part of the NATO 'Crusader' exercise, to evaluate the
effects of a nuclear attack on Britain.[10] In this exercise 125
nuclear weapons with a total yield of about 200 megatons
were assumed to have exploded over the UK (see Figure 7).
It is of course unlikely that a real attack would follow the
pattern of this exercise in detail; nevertheless the exercise
probably represents a reasonable estimate of likely targets
in a limited-scale nuclear attack on this country. According
to the Home Office publication *Domestic Nuclear Shelters:
Technical Guidance*, it is thought that in a nuclear war the
UK might expect an attack of 200 megatons.[11] This may be
an under-estimate. Mr Geoffrey Pattie, Secretary of State for
Defence (Air Force), in a written reply to a question in the
House of Commons concerning the Government assessment of the expected scale of a nuclear attack, stated 'more

● Ground-burst
○ Air-burst

Fig. 7 Operation Square Leg (based on maps published in the *New Statesman*)

than 1,000 megatons would be needed to destroy the ground-launched Cruise missiles once they were dispersed'.[12]

We shall follow through the consequences of the Square Leg attack, concentrating on London. Unlike about 18 other cities – for example, Cardiff, Birmingham, Liverpool, Edinburgh, Glasgow, and Nottingham, which suffer direct hits – Inner London is not hit directly. Five targets in or around the periphery of the London area are hit: Heathrow (two bombs, one a 1-megaton ground-burst and the other a 2-megaton air-burst); Brentford (a 2-megaton ground-burst); Croydon (a 3-megaton ground-burst); Potters Bar (a 3-megaton air-burst); and Ongar (a 2-megaton air-burst). These bombs are assumed to have exploded during the afternoon of Thursday 19 September. Southerly winds are prevailing. Within just a few hours, London is subjected to a release of explosive energy equivalent to about twice that released by all combatants during the five years of the Second World War.

☐ How war might break out: the pre-attack period

January–August 1980

In the Square Leg simulation, Warsaw Pact forces start to mobilise in January 1980. By April the USSR demands Norwegian and Danish withdrawal from NATO. The tension grows until, during August, the NATO commanders proclaim a state of military vigilance in anticipation of war. Reserves and US reinforcements are mobilised. In addition to the military preparations, covert civil preparations for war are now made. Key personnel, such as specialists and senior administrators, are dispersed to various centres which are supposed to be relatively secure from attack. For higher-level officials these centres are well-protected bunkers, but some borough centres are only hastily converted local authority buildings. The largely voluntary UK Warning and Monitoring Organisation

(UKWMO), which exists to give warning of attack and subsequently to monitor fall-out from its 873 monitoring posts, is mobilised. The Wartime Broadcasting Service (WTBS) is set up and Police Support Units of about 40 men are allocated to guard key centres.[13]

Local authorities become increasingly involved in the preparations as staff are rapidly briefed about the role they have been allotted both before and after an attack. In general these people have not been previously informed about this. Problems may arise if these staff do not agree to their allocated role and prefer to stay at home to help their families and friends. Such problems are likely to become increasingly acute as the attack becomes imminent.

August–September 1980

Preparations for war now become publicly apparent, as some services and supplies are dispersed away from likely target areas. In London, equipment and selected staff of the London fire brigade are moved out of the city. Hospital staff within a 15-mile radius of Charing Cross are moved out, leaving only a skeleton service. Most patients are sent home. Some public buildings such as schools or libraries are provided with some protection against blast and fall-out and with communication facilities so that they can act as wartime control centres. Earth is piled up against walls. Power generation and cooking and waste-disposal facilities are improvised, and a store of food and water made. Local authorities generally have small food reserves for emergencies, usually held within the school meals service. These supplies are reserved primarily for the staff in wartime centres.

British Airways and nationalised shipping are taken over. On 27 August the Government puts into motion preparations to remove art treasures from London.

On 12 September the Cabinet approves Queen's Order 2 (suspension of Parliament and the assumption of emergency powers). This effectively allows the Government to take any measures it deems necessary. This measure is followed by panic buying in the shops. Around the same time, the Prime Minister speaks to the nation on TV and Radio. A massive public information programme begins with pre-recorded instructions on how to prepare for a nuclear attack and with the distribution of pamphlets such as *Protect and Survive* and *Domestic Nuclear Shelters* .

□ Government advice before the attack

It is Government policy to discourage the evacuation of urban areas. Their argument is that the fall-out distribution will be unpredictable and will cover most of the country: 'No part of the United Kingdom can be considered safe from both the direct effects of the weapons and the resultant fall-out.' (*Protect and Survive*).[14] Clearly the Government would also wish to ensure a minimum of dislocation so that their preparations can be carried out efficiently. They have no desire to control and provide for refugees fleeing from the cities into the surrounding countryside. To quote an internal Home Office circular: 'There would be no question of implementing emergency feeding arrangements during the pre-attack period for those persons who chose to ignore the government's advice to stay in their own homes';[15] and from *Protect and Survive*: 'If you leave, your local authority may need to take your empty house for others to use.'[14] It seems likely that in reality many people may attempt to leave obvious targets such as major centres of population and areas close to military bases despite Government advice to stay put. Indeed in the Square Leg simulation large numbers of people were assumed to have fled Birmingham. They were lucky to have done so because it suffered a direct hit. Only minor roads could be used by those leaving because major roads are designated Essential Service Routes (ESRs). The 14 major roads leaving London are designated ESRs and reserved solely for Government traffic (see Figure 8).

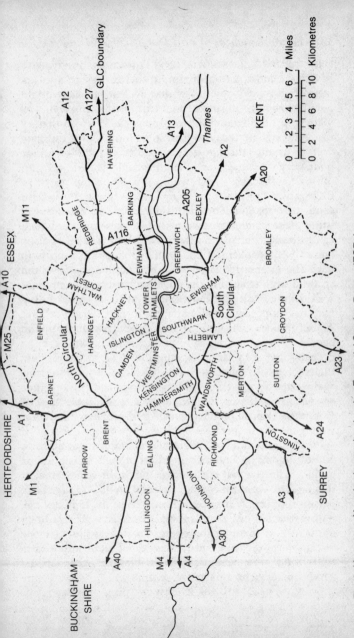

Fig. 8 Key map of London boroughs showing Essential Service Routes (ESRs)

Domestic Nuclear Shelters and *Protect and Survive* give advice on construction of simple shelters which are supposed to provide some protection against radioactive fall-out. If you have a garden, an earth shelter dug about 18 inches into the ground is recommended. Provided that all the materials are ready to hand the Home Office estimate that it would take two strong adults about 24 working hours each to make one. Many people would run into difficulties because there would not be enough earth in their gardens, or, since the water table is near the surface in some parts of London, their shelters might fill up with water. *Protect and Survive* also describes shelters which can be built inside the house. A basement is the best place but only 3½ per cent of London's population has access to one. The alternative is to use a ground-floor room or the space under a table or under doors propped against an inner wall. These shelters need covering with as much heavy material as possible and fastening to make them secure. These arduous preparations would be difficult for many people.

People living in caravans, bungalows, or on the top few floors of blocks of flats where there is little protection against radiation could only move out and 'make other arrangements'. Since they would assume that their chances of survival depend on having a shelter, people without one would become desperate.

Protect and Survive advises each family to make a 'fall-out room' in the innermost part of their house, and to build a primitive fall-out shelter (the 'inner refuge') inside this fall-out room away from external walls.[14] It says each person should stay inside the inner refuge for 48 hours and within the fall-out room for up to 14 days. The fall-out room should therefore be equipped with stocks of food, water, warm clothing, medicines, candles, an improvised toilet, and other essentials to enable the occupants to survive unaided for this length of time.

Everyone needs to drink at least two pints of water a day,

so a family of four must store a minimum of 14 gallons. We shall show in a later section (page 57) that in the conditions after nuclear attack far more than two pints a day would be necessary and that this store would be inadequate.

As for the problem of food, only foods which keep well and can be eaten cold should be stored, as there will be no power for cooking and refrigeration in the shelter. The food should be tinned or wrapped well to minimise contamination by radioactive dust. By considering the turnover times of food stocks in supermarkets and warehouses we estimate that there would be just enough food to go round provided that it was evenly distributed. But in the tense pre-attack period there would certainly be panic buying, hoarding, and sharply rising prices. The Ministry of Agriculture, Fisheries and Food has the legal power to intervene with control measures, but they are unlikely to be effective, particularly when most of their attention would necessarily be focused elsewhere. As Home Office internal circular ES1/79[15] says: 'Food would be scarce and no arrangements could ensure that every surviving household would have, say, 14 days' supply of food after attack.' These comments apply equally well to other supplies required for the shelter, such as disinfectant, polythene bags, buckets, and batteries. As usual, the poor, the elderly, and the disabled would suffer more in such circumstances.

Many people will be in no position to construct a shelter or obtain sufficient supplies. There will be a very strong temptation for them to steal supplies or to try to use other people's shelters. It is therefore no surprise that law and order is a top priority for the Government. This is the task of the police, though the army will be used when necessary. Fines and imprisonment are unlikely to be an effective deterrent in the face of impending nuclear war and stronger measures will have to be used. We cannot know whether the police and the army will attempt to stamp out all disturbances or just ensure that Government preparations and key sites are not interfered with. Even in those areas where order is still maintained, there will be many people who without help can neither understand nor act upon the Government's advice. War Emergency Plans and Home Office circulars recognise this and suggest that local authorities' social services departments should help them. In view of the scale of the problem, the large number of extra duties an already stretched service would have, and absenteeism, it is very unlikely that much help could be given.

In Government publications the image is given of a population quietly and efficiently preparing for war. Is this picture plausible? There will be shortage of supplies, jammed roads as people try to flee the cities, and public alarm at the prospect of a nuclear attack. There may be considerable panic and civil unrest.

In contrast, official unpublished documents take this into account and outline special measures to be undertaken by the police, primarily 'the detention or restriction of movement of *potentially* subversive people'[16] (our emphasis). It is not at all clear who this means. Under conditions of extreme tension this may include many ordinary people.

Of course one should bear in mind that there may well be a far shorter time between public warning and an attack than was envisaged in Square Leg. This is partly because 'warning of the necessity for covert preparation for war [is] likely to be delayed as long as possible',[16] presumably in order not to precipitate an attack. An example of this policy occurred during the 1962 Cuba Missile Crisis, when British civil defence was not mobilised for fear of provoking a Soviet pre-emptive attack.[17] There may even be no warning period of tension at all: for example, an attack may start by accident owing to a computer or system failure.

In any case, because of the extremely high speeds of ballistic missiles there may be as little as four or five minutes between the detection of a missile at take-off or in flight and its arrival. Even if people had proper shelters, in most cases they would not have enough time to reach them.

□ The Attack

In Operation Square Leg war was declared on 15 September. On Thursday 19 September there was an 'Attack Warning Red' at 11.55 a.m. followed by a first strike on the UK between noon and 12.10, and a second between 1.00 and 3.00 p.m.

The period between declaration of war and nuclear attack could well have been rather shorter. Indeed Home Office circular ES1/81 states, 'For planning purposes, it should be assumed that there may be as little as 7 days' warning of an attack and the basic essentials of plans should be capable of implementation in 48 hours.'[18]

In the following detailed description of the effects of the Square Leg attack on London we will assume that most people are at home and in some sort of shelter. The consequences are appalling even given these very optimistic assumptions.

□ Detailed consequences in the London area

No detailed analysis of the civil defence aspects of Square Leg has yet been published by the Government, despite the declared intention of the Home Secretary to make the information public.[19] We have therefore used the same conditions as in Square Leg to find out what would happen to London. We relate our findings to specific boroughs within the Greater London Council (GLC) area, an area some 25 miles across and with about 7 million inhabitants. Although London is used as the basis of this study the results are generally applicable to any city suffering a nuclear attack.

The maps (Figures 9 to 12) show the results of this nuclear attack. The same blast pressure rings are shown as in the one-megaton example but scaled where necessary for larger bombs and for different altitudes of detonation (see Appendix 1 for scaling laws).

Blast

Except for a mere 2 per cent, the whole GLC area is subjected to blast pressures greater than 1 p.s.i. Blast damage is therefore extensive. It is very doubtful that any windows would still be intact in the capital. Table 4 shows the areas affected by various blast levels and the resulting deaths and injuries. For a breakdown of casualties by borough see Table 5.

Sixteen per cent of London's population is killed and 36 per cent injured by the effects of blast alone. In blast damage Zone B, containing over a million people, a high proportion of survivors are trapped under houses. The prospects of these people surviving the next few days are bleak because outside help will not be available. Many will die and add to the total blast casualties.

Apart from killing and injuring people the blast causes

Table 4 Deaths and injuries resulting from blast

Blast zone	Blast pressure (p.s.i.)	Percentage of GLC area	Dead	Injured	Uninjured by blast
A	12 or more	8	401,000	8,000	—
B	5–12	21	567,000	453,000	113,000
C	2–5	46	167,000	1,506,000	1,674,000
D	1–2	23	—	512,000	1,313,000
outside D	less than 1	2	—	—	154,000
			Total 1,135,000	2,481,000	3,354,000

Note: These figures are calculated using 1977 census figures where the total resident population of London was 6,970,000 people.
Figures are rounded to the nearest thousand.

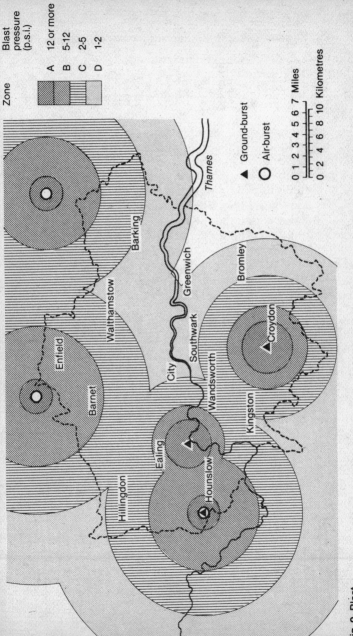

Zone		Blast pressure (p.s.i.)
A		12 or more
B		5-12
C		2-5
D		1-2

▲ Ground-burst

○ Air-burst

0 1 2 3 4 5 6 7 Miles
0 2 4 6 8 10 Kilometres

Fig. 9 Blast

Table 5 Casualties in Square Leg for each London borough

| | Blast casualties | | | Total casualties from blast and radiation | | | | | | Total population |
| | | | | Lower PF | | | Upper PF | | | |
	Dead	Injured	Uninjured	Dead	Injured	Uninjured	Dead	Injured	Uninjured	
City of London	—	1,400	4,200	5,600	—	—	5,600	—	—	5,600
Barking	1,100	43,000	109,000	1,100	43,000	109,000	1,100	43,000	109,000	153,000
Barnet	72,000	125,000	95,000	269,000	8,200	15,000	227,000	28,000	38,000	292,000
Bexley	—	27,000	188,000	—	27,000	188,000	—	27,000	188,000	215,000
Brent	16,000	115,000	125,000	256,000	—	—	228,000	9,800	18,000	256,000
Bromley	33,000	102,000	158,000	119,000	47,000	126,000	80,000	69,000	144,000	293,000
Camden	6,600	74,000	109,000	189,000	—	—	183,000	2,000	4,000	189,000
Croydon	241,000	58,000	23,000	300,000	9,600	12,000	298,000	11,000	13,000	322,000
Ealing	146,000	95,000	51,000	292,000	—	—	286,000	1,900	3,600	292,000
Enfield	66,000	111,000	83,000	260,000	—	—	260,000	—	—	260,000
Greenwich	—	40,000	166,000	32,000	29,000	145,000	5,000	38,000	163,000	206,000
Hackney	3,800	64,000	127,000	194,000	—	—	194,000	—	—	194,000
Hammersmith	26,000	72,000	66,000	164,000	—	—	95,000	24,000	45,000	164,000
Haringey	11,000	103,000	114,000	228,000	—	—	228,000	—	—	228,000
Harrow	9,900	90,000	99,000	199,000	—	—	189,000	3,000	6,000	199,000
Havering	15,000	101,000	125,000	15,000	101,000	125,000	15,000	101,000	125,000	240,000
Hillingdon	74,000	94,000	61,000	229,000	—	—	217,000	4,100	7,700	229,000

Hounslow	139,000	49,000	12,000	189,000	8,200	2,900	181,000	15,000	4,100	200,000
Islington	4,800	61,000	102,000	168,000	—	—	168,000	—	—	168,000
Kensington and Chelsea	6,600	66,000	87,000	159,000	—	—	95,000	20,000	44,000	159,000
Kingston upon Thames	5,300	55,000	76,000	9,000	58,000	70,000	5,300	55,000	76,000	136,000
Lambeth	37,000	111,000	135,000	283,000	—	—	283,000	—	—	283,000
Lewisham	8,000	93,000	143,000	223,000	3,900	17,000	167,000	21,000	55,000	244,000
Merton	28,000	71,000	67,000	135,000	12,000	19,000	80,000	35,000	50,000	166,000
Newham	—	57,000	172,000	94,000	24,000	111,000	13,000	52,000	165,000	230,000
Redbridge	2,400	67,000	160,000	54,000	40,000	135,000	3,700	66,000	159,000	229,000
Richmond upon Thames	87,000	54,000	24,000	127,000	22,000	16,000	124,000	24,000	17,000	165,000
Southwark	7,400	74,000	143,000	224,000	—	—	224,000	—	—	224,000
Sutton	59,000	61,000	46,000	107,000	26,000	34,000	92,000	35,000	39,000	167,000
Tower Hamlets	11,000	38,000	113,000	150,000	—	—	118,000	5,400	27,000	150,000
Waltham Forest	—	100,000	111,000	222,000	—	—	168,000	19,000	35,000	222,000
Wandsworth	15,000	117,000	146,000	278,000	—	—	201,000	24,000	53,000	278,000
Westminster	2,200	61,000	146,000	175,000	5,900	29,000	66,000	31,000	113,000	210,000
Total for Greater London	1,135,000	2,481,000	3,354,000	5,351,000	464,000	1,155,000	4,503,000	765,000	1,702,000	6,970,000

Note: Figures are quoted to the nearest thousand or 2 significant figures whichever is more accurate.

very extensive material damage. As far out as Zone C – that is throughout 75 per cent of the GLC area – roads are blocked by collapsed houses, fallen telegraph poles, overturned cars, and other debris. Houses throughout 29 per cent of the GLC area are reduced to rubble and those in a further 46 per cent too badly damaged to be repairable under wartime conditions. To give more specific examples of damage, Richmond, Kew, and Chiswick bridges are down and the elevated section of the M4 near Brentford is blown away. Kew Gardens is now a blackened charred landscape.

Burns and fire

The number of people receiving burns depends on how many are in the open or near windows when the bombs explode, the type of clothing worn, and even their skin type (darker skins absorb more heat). It is therefore difficult to predict burns casualties accurately. But even if only one per cent of the population were exposed there would be at least 50,000 second and third degree burns cases in the GLC area. This number *alone* would overwhelm the *entire country's* special burns units. As no outside help can be expected for as long as two weeks after the attack, the severely burned will suffer a very painful death. If large numbers of people are caught in the open while attempting to flee the capital many more will die. Burns injuries are further complicated by other injuries such as cuts and broken limbs. People looking towards the flash are also blinded. Although this complete blindness may be only temporary, those affected do not know whether they are permanently blind or not. Permanent eye damage can be caused by retinal burns. In either case these people are much more vulnerable to further injury by fire or falling debris and will have difficulty finding shelter.

Fire damage is very severe. The fire-fighting services, however, are not to be used immediately after the attack. Much of the service has been withdrawn from London since the main concern is 'the preservation of the fire service for

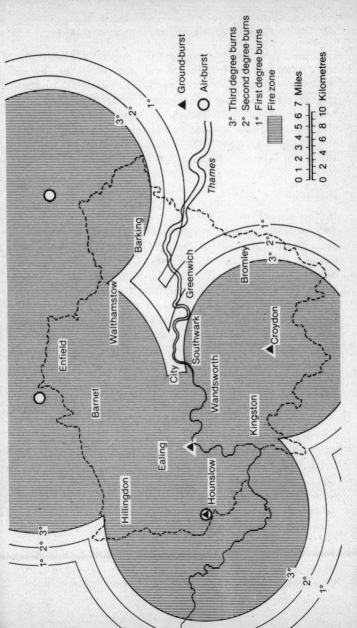

Fig. 10 Fire and burns

▲ Ground-burst
○ Air-burst

3° Third degree burns
2° Second degree burns
1° First degree burns
▨ Fire zone

0 1 2 3 4 5 6 7 Miles
0 2 4 6 8 10 Kilometres

Thames

Barking
Walthamstow
Enfield
Barnet
City
Hillingdon
Ealing
Greenwich
Southwark
Wandsworth
Bromley
Croydon
Kingston
Hounslow

its role in the longer survival period'.[20] Fires started all over
the capital (see Figure 10) will continue until they burn
themselves out. All of London may be destroyed in the
conflagration and many deaths and injuries are likely to
result. In our study, however, we have not included any
flash-burn or fire casualties because of the uncertainties in
estimating the numbers, but certainly hundreds of
thousands of deaths and injuries would be added to the final
totals.

Fall-out

In Square Leg the ground-burst explosions at Croydon,
Brentford, and Heathrow create mushroom-shaped clouds
10 to 20 miles across (see Figure 11). These clouds are blown
northwards by the wind, depositing fall-out as they go. In
most parts of London, survivors have less than half an hour
before fall-out arrives, to put out fires, crawl out from under
debris, and reconstruct their shelters. In the east of London,
survivors have rather longer (about four hours) before
fall-out arrives from the bomb on Eastbourne. These first
few hours or minutes are crucial. In over 50 per cent of the
GLC area an unprotected person receives a lethal dose of
radiation within six hours of the attack (within one hour in
boroughs such as Hillingdon, Ealing, and Southwark). The
total radiation dose an unprotected person receives over the
next two weeks is shown in Figure 12. The fall-out is spread
over very large areas of the capital. Here we have drawn
idealised cigar-shaped distributions of fall-out with none of
the 'hot spots' of radiation which are found in reality (see
pages 17–19). The actual radiation dose received by various
districts may well turn out to be different. Nevertheless,
the idealised contours shown give on average a reasonably
accurate indication of the overall situation (see Appendix
2).

Although most people receive most of their total radiation dose within the first few days, the resulting deaths
from radiation sickness do not occur until days or weeks

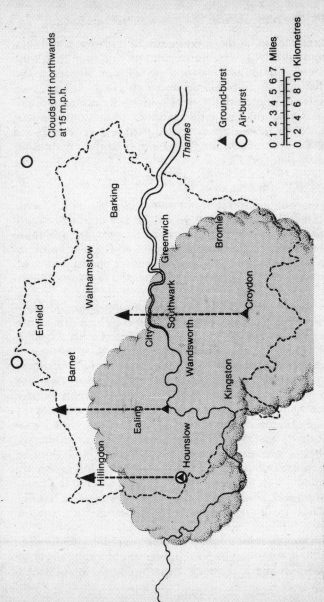

Clouds drift northwards at 15 m.p.h.

Barking

Walthamstow

Greenwich

Thames

Bromley

Croydon

Southwark

City

Enfield

Wandsworth

Barnet

Kingston

Hillingdon

Ealing

Hounslow

▲ Ground-burst

○ Air-burst

0 1 2 3 4 5 6 7 Miles

0 2 4 6 8 10 Kilometres

Fig. 11 Mushroom clouds

later. Details of the development of symptoms and of the times involved were shown previously in Table 3, page 20. Clearly almost all Londoners are radiation victims, unless they can protect themselves in effective shelters. Even outside the potentially lethal radiation zones almost every-body is affected by early symptoms of radiation sickness (anorexia, nausea, vomiting, and diarrhoea). Between 10 and 50 per cent of those receiving a dose of up to 200 rads suffer these symptoms.

Protection against fall-out

The radiation levels drawn on the map (Figure 12), while fatal for an unprotected person, do not necessarily prove fatal for someone in a shelter of some sort. For those without a purpose-built shelter Home Office advice is to stay indoors at home in a makeshift shelter with two weeks' supply of food and water. The Home Office pamphlet *Protect and Survive* gives advice on constructing a shelter from books, doors, tables, etc. According to *Domestic Nuclear Shelters: Technical Guidance*, however, neither a shelter like this, nor the makeshift garden shelter on page 32, could withstand a blast pressure of more than 1½ p.s.i.,[11] and consequently *would collapse in 85 per cent of the GLC area* (see Figure 9). *Domestic Nuclear Shelters:Technical Guidance* gives details of stronger shelters which cost more and take longer to construct. These are called the 'Indoor Kit Shelter', the 'Outdoor Kit Shelter', and the 'Purpose-Built Shelter'. The Indoor Kit Shelter is basically a steel box which has to be constructed by a specialist, at a cost of £500–£800 (1980 prices). To quote: 'it could be used for other purposes, e.g. as a workbench', (which gives an idea of its size). It is to be placed in the fall-out room and surrounded and covered with bricks, concrete blocks, or sandbags. About 3,300 bricks are needed for this: 'it takes four people approximate-ly 10 hours to carry 2,500 bricks from a stockpile and stack them around a shelter'. There would, however, be no

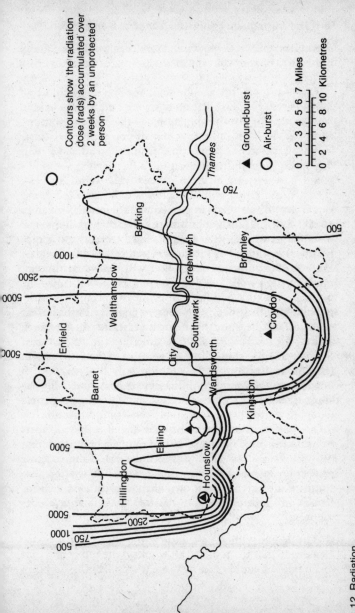

Fig. 12 Radiation

Contours show the radiation dose (rads) accumulated over 2 weeks by an unprotected person

▲ Ground-burst
○ Air-burst

0 1 2 3 4 5 6 7 Miles
0 2 4 6 8 10 Kilometres

stockpiles. Concrete blocks and sandbags would be equally difficult to obtain – but the instructions are 'install in crisis period'.

The next grade up, the Outdoor Kit Shelter, would cost £900–£1,800 plus installation costs. You dig a large hole in your garden (if you have one), place the shelter in it and cover it over. The leaflet says 'install in peacetime or crisis period', but later on: 'the time required to excavate will depend on your ability but with two fit people it should be possible to carry out all the necessary work within a week'.

Lastly, the Purpose-Built Shelter is to be installed in the garden by professionals in peacetime. The price is given as £6,000–£10,000 (current prices are rather higher). It must be installed in an area with good drainage – otherwise it may fill up with water. The kit shelters will collapse inside blast Zone B. The purpose-built shelter will withstand this but must be sited well clear (at least one and a half times the height) of nearby buildings to avoid the occupants being trapped by falling debris. In densely populated urban areas such as London, suitable sites are very rare. As explained above, the makeshift shelters described in *Protect and Survive* collapse throughout 85 per cent of the GLC area in the Square Leg attack. In addition only 3½ per cent of Londoners have access to a basement best suited for the simpler shelters.[21] In view of these difficulties most people would have to rely solely on their houses for protection.

One of the most important qualities of a shelter, apart from its resistance to blast, is its fall-out protection factor (PF, see page 22). Having examined the Home Office protection factors for houses and makeshift shelters, we compare the details of our own analysis with Home Office figures in Appendix 3, but the two main points are as follows:

● The Home Office calculations for the PF of a house assume that the roof and all windows are intact and that no fall-out could enter by these routes. This assumption is invalid for London where throughout the entire city virtually no window or roof would be intact after the Square Leg attack. Fall-out particles will enter houses and increase the dose of radiation received. Home Office PF values for an undamaged house therefore cannot be used.

● The Home Office calculations average out the thickness of the side of a house. In reality radiation more easily penetrates the thinner parts such as windows and doors. The larger amounts of radiation passing through these thinner sections must be taken into account. Because of this fact alone, Home Office PFs for undamaged houses are overestimates.

For many survivors the protection factor of a shelter is a rather academic point. Survivors inside damage Zone B have no home left nor any reasonable chance of reconstructing their shelter. They have little hope of avoiding a fatal

---

Protection factors

● In our calculations an upper and a lower value of protection factor have been used in each blast zone as follows:

Zone	Blast pressure (p.s.i.)	Protection factors Lower value	Upper value
A	12	1	1
B	5–12	1	2
C	2–5	2	5
D	1–2	5	10

The lower values of protection factors represent a reasonable estimate once blast damage is taken into account (see Appendix 3). The upper value is optimistic and discounts the majority of blast damage. In Zone D the value of 10 corresponds to a Home Office calculated value for an *undamaged* house (*Domestic Nuclear Shelters: Technical Guidance*).

---

radiation dose. They could try to leave the fall-out area if they were capable of moving, except that they would not know where to go, nor would they know if they were in a high fall-out zone. Only purpose-built shelters would be of any use. Inside Zones C and D, houses have damaged roofs, cracked walls, and smashed windows. Fall-out particles easily enter such a shelter. Even in the areas of lightest damage in London (outside Zone D) fall-out enters through broken windows.

Casualties due to fall-out in the GLC area

Calculating casualties from fall-out is a complex task because of the different protection factors which must be applied in each blast-damage zone. Also, people already injured by blast or burns are much more susceptible to radiation. Full details of our calculations are given in Appendix 4.

The effects of radiation add many more casualties because large areas of London are exposed to extremely high cumulative doses of radiation. For example, about one-fifth of the GLC area is exposed to over 6,000 rads within two weeks of the attack. Even if the effects of blast in reducing protection factors are neglected and a Home Office calculated PF of 10 is used, over one million people still receive a fatal dose of 600 rads or more. Once the effects of blast and injury are taken into account this figure is much higher. Within two weeks of the attack about 4 million people have received a fatal dose of radiation and are either dead or will die in the weeks ahead. Out of these 4 million casualties about half a million people receive very high but not immediately fatal doses of radiation and will take a long time to die. These unfortunate people can only be described as the 'living dead', but until they die they will be indistinguishable from less severe cases of radiation illness.

Total casualties

The total casualties about two months after the attack,

taking into account only blast and radiation, are given in Table 6. Figures in (a) have been calculated using the lower PF values, and in (b) the optimistic upper values.

Table 6 Total casualties in the GLC area

Dead	Injured	Uninjured by blast or radiation
(a) 5,351,000	464,000	1,155,000
(b) 4,503,000	765,000	1,702,000

These casualty figures are difficult to grasp because of their sheer magnitude, but it is a little easier if you take an example of 14 people you know. On average, immediately after the attack, two of your friends will be dead and five injured, of which one may be alive but trapped under rubble. One more may be so severely burned that he or she will soon die. A further six will be unhurt by blast but will be in danger from fires started by intense heat. Within a few days or so of the attack all your surviving friends will probably be suffering from nausea and vomiting caused by the symptoms of early radiation sickness. Within two weeks eight of your surviving friends will have received a fatal dose of radiation and will die over the next few weeks. Those injured or trapped under a house will die earlier. So after two months, neglecting the effects of fire, four of your friends may be alive. More probably only two or three will survive once the effects of fire are taken into account. Even this gloomy picture ignores all the other problems that would be experienced over the months following the attack and which are described in the next chapter, so these figures must be regarded as conservative estimates.

A fairly clear picture of casualties also emerges by looking at some London boroughs as examples (see Table 5, page 38). As one would expect, it is in boroughs nearer to the ground zeros that blast casualties are highest. Boroughs such as Hounslow and Croydon suffer badly in this respect.

Other boroughs with relatively light blast damage suffer huge casualties due to radiation. Lambeth and Islington, for example, are subjected to a cumulative dose of over 10,000 rads (20 times the lethal dose). Only those in a purpose-built underground shelter could survive such radiation levels. The most disturbing and insidious aspect of radiation sickness is that people do not know whether or not they have received a fatal dose. Millions of people could live for weeks in extreme suffering waiting to see if they would die. It should also be realised that many casualties would occur *outside* the GLC area, which we have not taken into account in this study.

☐ Life in the shelter

Let us consider the case of a family of four, which has improvised a shelter, managed to obtain supplies for 14 days, generally followed the Home Office advice given in *Protect and Survive* and survived the immediate effects of the attack with shelter intact – although the chances of a family managing to get this far are remote. Insurmountable problems may arise before the attack with food shortages; during the attack from blast and fire; and afterwards from radiation. However, it is important to find out what conditions would be like for any survivors outside blast and fire damage zones.

Our family of four are advised to remain inside their inner refuge for at least two days. Conditions are very cramped; they will have water, boxes of food, an improvised toilet, a first-aid kit, radio, blankets, and warm clothing. If they have taken the advice seriously they will also have taken in toys and games to pass the time. Somehow on top of all this they must fit themselves in (see Figure 13).

There is likely to be at least one injured person in each shelter. Many will die from complications arising from a combination of relatively minor injuries even though each individual injury would not normally be fatal.

As time progresses the shelter inhabitants receive an increasing dose of radiation. The earliest stages of radiation sickness begin with nausea, vomiting, and diarrhoea (see Table 3, page 20). Even at comparatively low doses below 200 rads, a significant number of people show these symptoms. In these conditions, because of the resulting dehydration, the recommended drinking water allocation is inadequate. Sanitation becomes of critical importance. In such cramped conditions it is impossible to avoid contact

Fig. 13 The *Protect and Survive* shelter

with excrement and vomit. The smell alone probably causes those not suffering from radiation sickness, especially children, to feel nauseated or to vomit. In these unhygienic conditions it is virtually impossible to keep anything clean: contamination of utensils, and, even more importantly, of wounds, is unavoidable. Large quantities of uncontaminated water, far in excess of that recommended, would be required.

Radiation drastically reduces the body's resistance to infection. Bacteria and viruses are, however, extremely resistant to radiation. As a result, the people in the shelter are likely to develop ailments such as gastro-enteritis or measles, and respiratory infections such as acute colds, bronchitis, or pneumonia. These ailments alone could prove fatal. Isolated in their shelter, they cannot judge whether their sickness or diarrhoea is caused by gastro-enteritis, acute psychological shock, or a potentially fatal radiation dose.

Survivors in the shelter are likely to suffer extreme psychological stress following a nuclear attack. The concern over any missing family members and friends, the lack of outside information during the communications blackout, and the feeling of nausea and claustrophobia will all combine to produce fear or uncontrolled terror, and a complete loss of any sense of reality. A death inside the shelter will cause enormous emotional stress, especially as radiation levels outside may be too high to allow the survivors to bury the corpse. Because of the greater vulnerability of children to radiation many adults will watch their children die before they themselves are affected. *Protect and Survive* merely advises that the body be placed in another room, covered securely, and identification attached.[14] Another factor contributing to psychological stress is the very real threat of violence from groups outside desperately seeking food, water, or shelter. Maintenance of security has to remain the responsibility of the individuals in the shelter. They certainly cannot just ring for the police.

Despite the dangers from radiation and from other survivors, trips outside the shelter to look for food and fresh water and to remove waste may soon become unavoidable, however hazardous. It is also possible that conditions inside the shelter will become so intolerable that some may find the outside preferable, even knowing full well that they will receive an increased dose of radiation. Inevitably fall-out will be brought into the shelter and contaminate remaining food and water. Fall-out will also drift in on air currents. Because of this, the level of radiation inside the shelter will rise, as will the risk of breathing in and eating or drinking radioactive particles.

The map of London after the attack (Figure 12) shows that, because of fall-out, there are few areas where our family in an improvised shelter could survive the two-week shelter period. Also, in many areas a two-week shelter

---

When is it safe to come out?

● It is Home Office policy to give the 'all-clear' message in a locality when the radiation level has fallen to a dose rate of ½ rad per hour. This figure is calculated on the assumption that people would still spend 6 to 8 hours inside every day so that the daily dose would not exceed 10 rads, which is assumed to be the body's recuperation rate. Although this dose is considered to be 'safe' and the all-clear would be given at this point, this *daily* dose of radiation is higher than the permitted *yearly* dose for radiation workers in peacetime, and the accumulated dose of several days working in the open air is certainly large enough to cause sterility and damage to the bone-marrow.[7]

Figure 14 shows how long it takes for the level of radioactivity to fall to this 'safe' level in the Greater London area after the Square Leg attack. One should bear in mind that few of the people sheltering inside the 17-day contour lines will survive, because their overall accumulated dose during the shelter period and after will be enough to kill them. The map also implies that it will not be safe for rescue workers to enter or pass through large areas of London until well over a month after the attack – a factor which would seriously hamper any attempts at recovery.

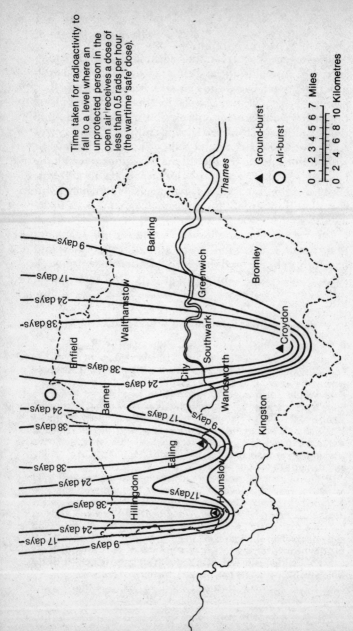

Time taken for radioactivity to fall to a level where an unprotected person in the open air receives a dose of less than 0.5 rads per hour (the wartime 'safe' dose).

▲ Ground-burst
○ Air-burst

0 1 2 3 4 5 6 7 Miles
0 2 4 6 8 10 Kilometres

Fig. 14 'When is it safe to come out?'

period would not be long enough. Over a large area of London, radiation would be so high that it would take much longer than two weeks for the dose rate to fall to ½ rad per hour (the wartime 'all-clear' dose rate). For 15 per cent of London – over a million people – the wait for the 'all-clear' would be over five weeks (see Figure 14). In these areas survivors after two weeks are still supposed to restrict visits outside severely. In practice, where the wait would be very long the radiation levels would be high enough to kill anyway and the 'all-clear', if it sounded at all, would be an ironic message delivered to corpses or those already dying from radiation sickness.

Millions of Londoners, who sheltered and followed Government advice in boroughs such as Lambeth, Southwark, Islington, Haringey, Ealing, Harrow, Hillingdon, or Hackney would receive a lethal dose more slowly than those who took no precautions at all. In this case taking Government advice would be worse than taking none at all because one would simply be delaying the inevitable for a few miserable weeks.

☐ Summary

- In the context of the Square Leg attack on London the advice in *Protect and Survive* is worthless, unless you are lucky enough to be outside the main fall-out area or have access to really effective shelter – which means going underground for several weeks.
- The advice given by the Home Office is based on faulty assumptions which lead to overestimates of the protection given by buildings.
- Even in the Square Leg attack, in which no bomb falls on Inner London, over one million die in seconds from blast injuries and more than 4 million from radiation over a period of up to two months after the attack. At least half a million people are injured by blast. About one million Londoners survive uninjured by blast. Many of these suffer burns or non-fatal radiation sickness.

Life in
the
Aftermath

The Home Office has provided little information for the
public about what life will be like after the shelter period.
Protect and Survive simply says, 'on hearing the all
clear . . . you may resume normal activities'.[14] In this
chapter we examine what 'normal activities' will mean for
a Londoner.

A survivor emerging for the first time from the shelter
will find the outside world in utter chaos: roads blocked by
overturned cars and fallen telegraph poles; bricks, roofing
tiles and broken glass everywhere; a smell of burning in the
air from smouldering fires all over the city; and the stench
of putrefying bodies lying where they have fallen or been
thrown by the blast.

All the services we rely on today will, if they are running
at all, be very limited. There will be no piped water, no
sewage disposal system, no food in the shops, no heating or
lighting, little or no medical care, no telephones or postal
system. Money will have no value. Law and order will have
broken down and martial law will be in force. Survivors will
also face the inescapable dangers of radiation.

□ Water

Most survivors will be suffering from radiation sickness,
untreated injuries, or illnesses arising from unhygienic

living conditions. As a consequence, excessive body-water loss from vomiting, diarrhoea, or fever will more than double their water requirements from about two pints to four pints or more per day. Thirst may well drive people out of their shelter even before the 'all-clear' sounds.

London's water services

● London's water services are largely the responsibility of the Metropolitan Water Division of the Thames Water Authority. The division extracts over 400 million gallons of water each day, principally from the river Thames (73%), the river Lea (14%), and from wells and springs in the Lea valley, Kent, and Surrey (13%). The river water is pumped into one or other of 34 storage reservoirs, purified, and then pumped into the distribution systems. Figure 15 shows the location of the main reservoirs, treatment stations, and sewage works which serve Greater London.

In the Square Leg attack, the reservoirs in the West London chain, together with their associated treatment works and pumping stations, are within blast-damage Zone B. These blast pressures are sufficient to ensure the destruction of all the buildings on these sites and to cause severe damage to equipment. Depending on the exact point of impact of the warheads, some of the reservoirs may be breached and the Staines aqueduct damaged beyond repair. Particularly serious is the loss of Ashford Common, Hampton, and Kempton treatment works since they supply London with two-thirds of its water supply.

In North London the reservoirs, pumping stations, and the Coppermills treatment works in the Lea Valley are within blast-damage Zone C. The blast would damage equipment but, in principle, the damage would be repairable. All this area, however, would receive very high levels of fall-out from Croydon, hindering any repair operation for at least a month. Those facilities escaping blast damage would not stay in operation long since 'even in peacetime water systems are kept in operation only by regular maintenance'.[22] Little maintenance or repair work would be possible after the attack because of lack of available skilled staff (many killed, injured, or simply unwilling to leave their families), scarce piping and other material stocks, and high levels of radiation preventing staff from surveying the damage.

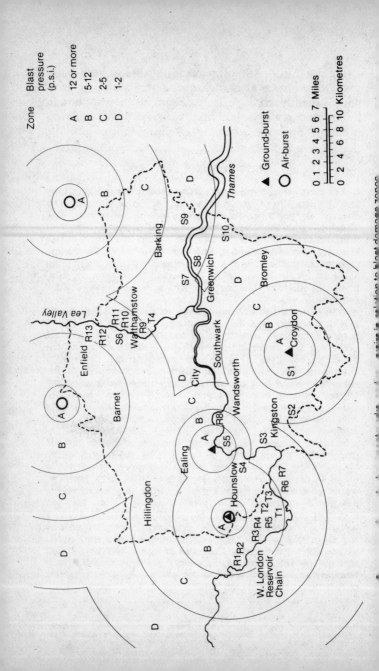

Zone	Blast pressure (p.s.i.)
A	12 or more
B	5–12
C	2–5
D	1–2

▲ Ground-burst
○ Air-burst

Miles 0 1 2 3 4 5 6 7
Kilometres 0 2 4 6 8 10

In the Square Leg attack, the major elements of the water supply system are extensively damaged. The only remaining uncontaminated source of drinking water is from any accessible and undamaged artesian wells. If about half of these remain operational there will be *just* enough drinking water (at two pints a day) for about 2½ million people *provided that* this water can be distributed.

Once the piped water distribution system has collapsed the fire service is responsible for distributing any available water. In practice, distribution will be very difficult because of street blockages and the small numbers of suitable vehicles available for carrying water. Water will not run from domestic water taps for a long time. Indeed as Home Office internal circular ES6/76 states: 'It can be said with absolute assurance that any widespread nuclear attack would quickly disrupt the distribution system for domestic and industrial water and much of the sewerage system.'[22]

In these circumstances it is very likely that water held in the reservoirs in north London, in the Lea Valley, and in the New River will have to be used. This water is likely to be contaminated by fall-out. Some isotopes like iodine-131, tritium, and strontium-90 dissolve in water and pose grave health hazards. The Home Office disregards these hazards: 'The contamination of drinking water by radioactive material does not add significantly to the dangers which would

Sewage		Reservoirs		Treatment Works	
S1	Croydon	R1	Queen Mother	T1	Ashford Common
S2	Worcester Park	R2	Wraysbury	T2	Kempton Park
S3	Kingston	R3	King George VI	T3	Hampton
S4	Isleworth	R4	Staines	T4	Coppermills
S5	Richmond	R5	Queen Mary		
S6	Enfield	R6	Queen Elizabeth II		
S7	East Ham	R7	Island Barn		
S8	Abbey Wood	R8	Barn Elms		
S9	Rainham	R9	Walthamstow		
S10	Dartford	R10	Lockwood		
		R11	Banbury		
		R12	William Girling		
		R13	King George's		

already exist from concurrent environmental radiation.'[22] Initially, such contaminated water does pose a lesser hazard than disease and radiation. Drinking this water, however, will result in an additional source of radiation inside the body, and will consequently lead to a higher incidence of deaths from radiation.

Water supplies will also be in danger of contamination by bacteria from the collapse of the sewage and waste-disposal systems. Widespread disease may result, as has been found after other disasters such as earthquakes.

Despite the longer-term dangers from drinking contaminated water, the most pressing need for survival is for water of *any* sort. Survivors can live for only a few days at most after running out of water. Water distribution and supply will, however, be at a standstill immediately after the shelter period – just when water has run out and is most needed. For this reason surviving Londoners could die of thirst before ever encountering any longer-term dangers.

☐ Food

There are major shortages both in the short and long term. Government plans assume that people have 14 days' supply of food in their shelter. But before the attack many will not have been able to stock up enough for 14 days because of shortages, panic buying, rapidly rising food prices, or simply insufficient warning. As a consequence many people will certainly go hungry. In the longer term there will be no significant imports of food since every major sea and air port has been destroyed. In any case our major suppliers are also likely to have suffered nuclear attacks. The country will have to survive on remaining stocks.

Food stocks

Some food supplies will be available from the national stockpile dispersed under the control of the Ministry of Agriculture, Fisheries and Food. This stockpile is held in depots throughout the country and will be under the control of regional government after the attack. If there is enough time, local councils will also have attempted to build up stockpiles from wholesale buffer stocks in the pre-attack period. As an example, details of Watford's planned stores (located less than two miles from North-wood NATO naval command HQ) are given in Table 7. These stores, even if they were obtained, would be sufficient to supply the public for only 14 days and the depots would not be very secure. One of the possible 'depots' is a lock-up garage, a structure which would not resist blast pressure or prevent contamination by fall-out.

Food could be requisitioned from local stocks in super-markets, warehouses, and food manufacturing or processing plants. But not much food will remain in retail and wholesale stores, since most of it will have been sold in the pre-attack period.

In London the food industries are strongly concentrated in the inner northern and north-western areas (Camden, Haringey, Barnet, Hackney, etc.) where the highest fall-out levels occur in Square Leg. Blast pressures in the 2–5 p.s.i. range have shattered windows and ripped off roofs, allowing fall-out to penetrate buildings. These food stocks are therefore in some of the last areas to become accessible and the food they contain may well be highly contaminated.

Some food may be salvaged but distribution is a major problem because of lack of fuel, the general blockage of roads, and dangerous levels of radiation. As time progresses and food runs out, shortages worsen. People starve. Limited amounts of food might be obtained from raiding the homes of the dead. Under these circumstances, severely contamin-ated food will almost certainly be eaten. Much food is contaminated by fall-out or spoilt in other ways. Food packaging is damaged by blast or by rain penetrating broken windows and roofs, increasing the risk of contamination by bacteria or fall-out. Frozen goods rot in their cold stores because of the inevitable loss of the power supply. Accord-ing to the Home Office publication *Nuclear Weapons*:

the protection afforded by the building and the containers themselves would normally be sufficient to reduce the amount of fall-out coming into contact with the stored food to such a low level that consumption of contaminated food would not result in a radiation dose to the gut in excess of 50 rads in one day.[23]

In fact this is an extremely high dose compared with the peacetime limit of 15 rads *per year* to a single organ for workers in the nuclear industry.

Apart from all the long-term dangers arising from eating radioactive matter, doses of over 50 rads per day may prove critical, even in the short term, for all those people who

---

Table 7 Watford's planned emergency food stocks

Addresses of stores

A. Cassio College of Further Education, Langley Road	Watford 24362
B. Watford Town Hall	Watford 26400
C. Town Hall, Lock up Garages	Watford 26400
D. Essex Hall, Town Hall	Watford 26400

Scale of county buffer ration deliveries pre-attack (14 days' supply)

Item	Individual ration	Total
Tea	3½ oz	7 tons 9 cwt
Sugar	14 oz	29 tons 16 cwt
Drinking Chocolate/Cocoa/ Ovaltine	7 oz	14 tons 18 cwt
Dry Biscuits	1¾ lbs	59 tons 7 cwt
Dried Milk	7 oz	14 tons 18 cwt
or		
Evaporated Milk	2 x 12 oz tins	152,800 tins
Potatoes	7 lbs	238 tons 14 cwt
or		
Rice/Pasta	1¾ lbs	59 tons 7 cwt
Fresh Root Veg	4 lbs	136 tons 8 cwt
or		
Tinned Veg	3½ lbs	119 tons 7 cwt
Tinned Meat/Fish	2 lbs	68 tons 4 cwt
Salt	4 oz	8 tons 10 cwt
Pepper	¼ oz	10 cwt

From Watford District War Emergency Plan.

have already received over 100 rads. The death rate increases sharply for total doses of between 200 and 400 rads (see Appendix 4, Figure 21).

Farming and food imports

Once all food stocks have been consumed, the only possible supplies of food are imports and home farming. It would be quite unrealistic to expect any significant levels of food imports for a long time. Starvation is the prospect facing survivors. Regional Controllers have to deny survivors food in order to retain sufficient seed grain and livestock to begin next year's agricultural production. In any case, a return to normal farming practices will not be possible. Most prime agricultural land in the UK will have experienced as high a level of radioactive contamination as the London area. Without adequate supplies of fertilisers or of oil to run machinery, modern farming technology cannot be used. The country will have to revert to more primitive farming methods for decades to come.

☐ Housing

After the Square Leg attack in September, survivors lucky enough to find adequate food and water are faced with the prospect of surviving a cold, wet winter without adequate shelter or heating. Cold will kill many people, particularly the very old and the very young who are particularly vulnerable to respiratory diseases and hypothermia.

Repairs to homes will be very limited. As Home Office circular ES3/76 states:

the repair of damaged houses would be restricted by the scarcity of all building materials and the demands of existing supplies for equally urgent tasks in essential industries and services. Such work as patching and weather proofing, done by self-help or perhaps by teams of volunteers organised by local authorities, would be dependent on the use of salvaged materials. Repairs would have to be confined to the more lightly damaged areas: any attempt to restore the more badly damaged towns and cities would be totally beyond the resources available, and the main activity in these areas, when radiological levels permitted movement into them, would be the salvaging of usable building materials.[24]

This is a truly bleak prospect for survivors in London and in the majority of towns and cities in Britain.

☐ Medical care

Our assessment of the Square Leg attack on the London area shows that surviving medical services are completely overwhelmed by the numbers of casualties involved. There are over 2 million people injured by blast in the London area alone, yet it is estimated that only 24,000 hospital beds out of 60,000 in the GLC area will be usable after the nuclear attack because of blast damage to hospital buildings.[25] The War Emergency Plans envisage evacuation of some in-patients and hospital facilities within a 15-mile radius of Charing Cross before an attack. In the Square Leg simulation this achieves nothing because most bombs fall around the periphery of the GLC area. In the aftermath many blast survivors will be dying from injuries and radiation sickness. Medical services will then need to cope with half a million people with blast injuries and a similar number of people with radiation sickness. Inevitably, many doctors will be among the dead and injured. At a generous estimate only about half of London's doctors (about 9,000) will survive and be capable of treating the sick and injured.

Because of the blockage of roads by debris, damage to vehicles, and the presence of radiation, it will be very difficult to transport patients to any remaining medical centres. In the face of scant medical services, doctors will be forced to be very selective about whom they treat. The 'triage' system will be adopted, in which casualties are classified into three categories:

● those unlikely to survive after available treatment

● those likely to survive after available treatment
● those likely to survive even without treatment.

Casualties in the first and third category will not be given any treatment. Health service plans state that 'People suffering from radiation sickness *only*, should not be admitted [to hospital]'[26] (our emphasis).

This system will present doctors with terrible moral and practical dilemmas. Without a thorough diagnosis it will be difficult to distinguish between radiation sickness of various doses, dysentery, gastro-enteritis, and stress. The injured and their families are unlikely to accept the doctors' decisions. Order in hospitals would be difficult to maintain without the police and military.

The four most important medical problems will be: burns, radiation sickness, multiple injuries, and extreme psychological shock. The treatment of severe burns requires extensive surgery over many months including the grafting of skin on to non-healing burns, the release of burn contractions, the removal of burn-induced tumours, and delicate plastic surgery. But even in peacetime no more than 100 acute burn cases can be handled in the whole of the UK simultaneously. In London *alone* after a nuclear attack there would be tens of thousands of people with burns.

Radiation further complicates injuries because it destroys white blood cells which normally guard against infection. Radiation also causes haemorrhages and eventually leads to the breakdown of bone marrow and soft tissue. Extensive blood transfusions will be required by many tens of thousands of people. This will not be possible because in London there are only about 5,000 pints of blood stored for emergency use (sufficient for about 2,500 blood transfusions). Moreover, much of this would be unusable, some of it having been destroyed directly by the blast, and more by the loss of power to cold stores in which it must be kept.

The treatment of radiation victims may pose unacceptable risks to the doctors. To quote from a case documented in the *New England Journal of Medicine*:

Even after thoroughly bathing the patient, those attendants who were exposed to his body at a distance of two feet for a period of nine hours received the maximum allowable radiation exposure for one week. All vomitus, feces and urine were contaminated with radioactive elements, presenting significant problems of disposal. All those attending the patient were required to wear caps, gowns, masks, plastic gloves and grocery sacks tied over their shoes.[27]

Another report quoting the case of a worker who received a dose of 200 rads in a laboratory accident in the USA showed that 47 days' intensive care was required.[28]

Patients who have suffered limb fractures, lung damage or multiple cuts require immediate surgery. Lack of staff, drugs, and anaesthetics will make this impossible.

Psychological problems are also very serious. This has been concisely summarised in the *British Medical Journal*:

After a large nuclear attack the psychological problems of a bombed population may create as many problems as the physical injuries, particularly as they may affect otherwise uninjured survivors on whom reconstruction will depend. Psychological reactions to the threat of attack, a period in the fall-out shelter, the large numbers of dead and injured who will not be rescued, and eventual emergence into a society where normal services and supplies are disrupted may well disable otherwise healthy survivors and hamper their efforts at recovery.[29]

To summarise, it is inconceivable that even one in every hundred of the millions injured or sick in the GLC area would receive proper treatment or pain-killers. As a result most of those in the second triage category, for whom treatment would mean the difference between life and death, might die. A study by some American doctors concluded: 'All thoughtfully acquired evidence overwhelmingly states that the medical response to nuclear weapon warfare will be desperately inadequate to the need.'[30] Indeed some doctors have suggested that a means of suicide might be the most 'humane' treatment that could be provided.

☐ Environmental health

In the unhygienic conditions after the attack 'Enteric [intestinal] infections ..., coupled with the lack of proper sanitary facilities, could spread rapidly to assume epidemic proportions.'[31] Hepatitis, typhoid, cholera, forms of dysentery, tuberculosis, and respiratory ailments (pneumonia, acute colds, and bronchitis) are all likely to occur. Rats and insects, who are much more resistant to radiation than human beings, will flourish among the debris and spread disease.

Millions of decomposing human and animal corpses lie buried under rubble and in buildings. They present a great health hazard and must be buried or incinerated as quickly as possible. This task, however, cannot be completed for many weeks because of the shortage of labour and difficulties in removing bodies. On account of the number of corpses, religious rites and the wishes of surviving relatives will have to be ignored (as stated in ES8/76).[31] Burial, where possible, will have to be in mass graves. Months and years after the attack unhygienic conditions, coupled with hunger and the low level of welfare services, mean that all the diseases mentioned above will become a permanent threat to survivors.

☐ Labour

In peacetime, British industry depends heavily not only on a large manual workforce, but also on high-technology equipment and a complex structure of skilled workers, engineers, and managers. The wholesale destruction of plant, the collapse of the power system, the acute scarcity of fuel, and the massive casualties amongst the population will bring industry to a standstill after an attack. There will be a severe shortage of skilled people able to reconstruct industry. In the aftermath the main demand will be for heavy manual labour for road clearance, emergency sanitation, and the burial of the dead. People may be reluctant or unable to undertake such heavy and unpleasant work. Regional commissioners will have statutory powers to direct labour but the difficulty will be to provide adequate incentives. Indeed as Home Office circular ES3/76 states:

in the absence of effective sanctions, *short of summary execution*, for dealing with those who might not comply with directions, success . . . would in practice depend on the community's acceptance of the need . . . The difficulty would be to provide incentives. Money would have no value, and initial rewards for labour might be a meal or extra food for the family.[24] [our emphasis]

It is hard to predict exactly how the population would react but with the combination of little food, disease, and the effects of radiation causing fatigue, malaise, and depression, typical responses are likely to vary from passive to active resistance to work.

☐ Law and order

After the attack, people may well have to take the law into their own hands simply to survive. Actions which in peacetime would be unacceptable, such as looting and violence, may become commonplace. Therefore 'maintenance of public order would be one of the essential tasks of wartime 'regional government', the responsibility for this falling on the police and armed forces backed up by a system of regional courts with emergency powers.[24]

To quote further from this Home Office circular:

In conditions in which death, destruction and injury were commonplace, such penalties as probation, fines or sentences of imprisonment would no longer be effective. Such penalties as communal labour, restricted rations and exposure to public disapproval might be appropriate for all but the gravest offences, but in the case of flagrantly anti-social behaviour there might be a need for harsher penalties than would be generally acceptable in peacetime . . . Regional Commissioners, acting through their commissioners of justice, would be empowered to impose such penalties as they thought fit in the light of conditions and circumstances at the time.[24]

People will have no control over these non-elected officials who will in effect have absolute power. Survivors may be forcibly transported from their homes to perform basic unfamiliar tasks with uncertain rewards. Human rights and freedoms accepted as normal in peacetime will have vanished. It is assumed throughout that the officials in control are capable of making rational decisions. This seems highly unlikely in view of the extreme circumstances involving personal loss and isolation from most of the perils facing survivors outside.

☐ Power, transport, and communications

In a nuclear war there will be large-scale disruption of all normal services over most of the country. In peacetime, disruption of any *one* of these can bring chaos and public outcry – witness for example the effects of strikes by power-station engineers.

Energy

In the London area most of the electricity-generating capacity is situated along the Thames to the east of the city[32] and in the Square Leg attack receives comparatively moderate blast pressures in the 1–2 p.s.i. range. These stations will therefore be repairable, provided that the necessary staff are available. Substations in west, outer south, and outer north London, however, are irreparably damaged, leaving large sections of the Greater London area without any hope of power, so most commercial and industrial activities, including the operation of water treatment works, will be disrupted. Over the whole country, blast will damage many electricity-generating stations and switching stations beyond repair. Pylons, overhead transmission lines, and many vital links in the national grid system will be broken. Radioactive fall-out dust will also damage insulators. Furthermore, if high altitude explosions (causing large Electro-Magnetic Pulses) are deliberately used as a strategy, the entire national grid could be made inoperative by the induction of excessive currents in the network of transmission lines. In the Square Leg exercise direct hits are made on nuclear power stations and reprocessing plants like Dungeness and Windscale. As these supply only about 10 per cent of our electricity (1.6 per cent of our total energy supply) their loss is of relatively minor importance. But the effects of the dispersal of their radioactive contents over wide areas creates an extremely serious long-term problem (see Appendix 5).

Gas distribution equipment, oil refineries, and storage installations will also be damaged seriously. Energy for the nation as a whole will be in extremely short supply. All remaining fuel stocks, including coal, oil, and petrol will be guarded by the police for use only by the authorities, as imports cannot be expected.

Transport and communications

The lack of fuel, the blocking of roads, the destruction of railway tracks, signalling equipment, and rolling stock will bring the national transport system to a virtual standstill. In the Square Leg attack, most destruction of transport occurs in the suburbs, wrecking the radial railway network and trunk roads. The Home Office emergency measures for transport include the following: 'The transport of essential supplies would present serious problems ... some use might be made of small boats and rafts propelled manually.'[24] Public transport will be non-existent and most people will be unable to move around the country to find out if their relatives and friends are still alive. Even if the telephone system is still working it will not be available for use. British Telecom has a 'Telephone Preference System' which enables them to disconnect rapidly over 90 per cent of users in a 'national emergency'.[33] All telephone users are currently placed in one of three categories and only 'important' individuals placed in the highest category would be 'on-line'. The net disruption of services and communications will therefore leave the surviving population isolated.

☐ The economy

Financial institutions, banks, Government agencies, companies, etc. all rely on centralised records and administration, and on effective communications with regional departments. Vital channels of communication and essential records will be destroyed in a nuclear attack. Money will no longer have any value, nor will credit cards or bank accounts. Any survivors will have to rely on primitive barter systems or just take what they need if it is available.

An important point is that one of the factors used in deciding nuclear missile targeting is the elimination of the economic recovery of an adversary in the long term. As the Chairman of the US Joint Chief of Staffs said in 1976, 'We do not target population per se any more. What we are doing now is targeting a war recovery capability.'[34]

A major problem for economic recovery after a nuclear attack – if it were at all possible – is to restart industry and agriculture in order to produce new goods before existing supplies run out. Certainly after an attack all air and sea ports will have been destroyed as well as the vast majority of our manufacturing ability. Large areas of farmland will be contaminated by radiation, and oil will not be available for powering agricultural machinery. In many ways society will resemble that of medieval times. If the survivors consume more than they produce, 'each postwar year would see a lower level of economic activity than the year before and the future of civilisation itself . . . would be in doubt'.[4]

☐ **Summary**

● Many people may die of thirst due to the disruption of the water distribution and supply network.

● The British Home Office underestimates the importance of most hazards from radiation in food or water. As a result of shortages many people will have to consume contaminated food or water.

● The food supply will be inadequate, and worsen as time goes on. Those surviving the blast, fire, and radiation may starve to death.

● Medical care will be hopelessly inadequate, leaving people to die a painfully lingering death from blast injuries, burns, or radiation sickness.

● Owing to the breakdown of public hygiene, epidemics may spread through the surviving population

● Cold will kill many people as they spend winter without adequate shelter.

● Martial law and extreme circumstances will mean the effective loss of most civil liberties.

● People will be isolated by an almost complete lack of normal communications.

Long-term Biological Hazards

The immediate effects of nuclear explosions are catastrophic and life in the aftermath harrowing and uncertain for any survivors. But apart from the destruction of society, nuclear war would have very damaging effects on the Earth's natural environment. The destruction and pollution of the environment, and the extent of disruption of delicate ecological systems are key factors in determining whether plants, animals, and human beings could survive after nuclear war. At the very least, the dispersal of fall-out around the globe would result in a higher than normal incidence of cancer amongst survivors both near to and far from the war zone. At worst, long-term environmental damage could be so severe that the survival of the human race would be doubtful.

☐ Delayed fall-out

Much of the radioactive debris from a nuclear bomb falls back to the ground in the first few hours after the explosion and causes extremely high levels of radioactivity near the explosion. In the following days dangerous levels of radioactivity are spread many miles downwind. This is the 'primary fall-out', which is responsible for a large proportion of the deaths in the first few weeks after the attack. Some of the radioactive dust, however, is carried high up into the stratosphere (a comparatively stable region of the atmosphere), where it can float for many months or even years before finally falling towards the ground again. This 'delayed fall-out' descends very slowly to lower levels in the atmosphere, where it can be brought down by rain. In ground-burst explosions, most radioactive debris falls to earth within a few days as primary fall-out and only about 40 per cent of it remains airborne for long periods.[5] For medium- to high-yield air-burst explosions most of the radioactive residue remains in the stratosphere for a long time. The time taken for this fall-out to reach the ground depends both on the altitude of the initial explosion and on the size of the fall-out particles. Extremely small particles with diameters of a few hundred-thousandths of an inch can remain suspended in the atmosphere for several years. During this period the dust can be blown many times round the world by strong winds in the upper atmosphere (in narrow regions called 'jet streams' the wind speed often exceeds 100 m.p.h.). Delayed fall-out may therefore be deposited on the ground thousands of miles from the explosion and up to several years after the attack.

Although primary fall-out and the associated high levels of radioactivity kill many millions of people in the first few weeks after the attack, there will still be some people who have avoided a fatal dose of radiation. For these people the long-term biological effects of their initial exposure to low levels of radiation and their slowly accumulating dose through delayed fall-out will lessen their chances of ultimate survival.

The most dangerous components of delayed fall-out are the long-lived radioactive isotopes strontium-90 and caesium-137, which have half-lives of 27.7 and 30 years respectively. (The half-life is the time taken for the radioactivity to drop to one half of its initial level.) These long-lived radioactive isotopes represent about 10 per cent of the total fission products of the bomb and when deposited on the land contaminate soil, crops, and water sources, producing a potential health risk. People can absorb this material in a number of ways: by breathing it in, absorbing it through wounds, eating contaminated crops,[35] eating the meat from grazing animals, and drinking contaminated water or milk. As an example of this, considerable concern was expressed in the UK during the early 1960s over high strontium-90 levels in cows' milk caused by nuclear weapon testing. Once deposited in the body these radioactive substances can be retained in the tissues and bones for years and, although they may not prove immediately fatal, the slow exposure to radiation of various vital organs poses a much longer-term health hazard.

☐ Long-term health problems

The most notable effect of low doses of radiation in the long term, whether acquired through immediate or delayed fall-out, is a higher incidence of cancer. The slow release of radiation from fall-out particles inside or outside the body gradually damages previous healthy cells so that they become cancerous and eventually develop into malignant tumours. Leukaemia (cancer of the blood) was the most common form of cancer in the few years immediately following attacks on Hiroshima and Nagasaki. Since then, while leukaemia has been on the decline amongst the survivors of the bombings, other forms of cancer have increased. As a result of Japanese investigations it has been found that cancers of the respiratory organs, digestive organs, breast, and thyroid glands, as well as leukaemia, can all be caused by low doses of radiation received during and after a nuclear explosion.[36] Children and developing foetuses are more susceptible to these effects than fully grown adults.[37] For every one million survivors exposed to a total dose of 100 rads, the long-term cancer incidence induced by radiation would be as follows:

Leukaemia	2,000 deaths
General cancer	10,500 deaths[38]

Compared to normal incidence, these figures represent about a 40 per cent increase in deaths from general cancer and an increase of over 100 per cent in deaths from leukaemia. Home Office figures in *Nuclear Weapons* are similar for leukaemia, but they expect about half the number of deaths from general cancer. For doses higher or lower than 100 rads the number of cases of cancer would increase or decrease respectively. The dose/incidence relationship is, however, somewhat uncertain.[6]

Another serious long-term biological hazard of radiation is that damage to DNA molecules, which carry the human genetic code in reproductive cells, can give rise to mutations so that babies conceived after the attack may be born with deformities. Data from Japan show that these deformities include mongolism, below-average head size, dislocation of limbs, funnel chest, and mental retardation.[36] One of the radioactive products of the initial explosion, carbon-14, is particularly dangerous in this respect. Carbon is one of the basic building blocks of all organic molecules making up the human body. DNA molecules for instance contain a large number of non-radioactive carbon-12 atoms. Carbon-14 atoms, however, have an extremely long half-life (5,730 years) and once taken into the body can replace the normal carbon-12 atoms in DNA, thereby damaging genes from within.

The long-term effects of radiation exposure may not be the only health problem that survivors would have to face in the months following a nuclear attack. Damage caused to buildings by nuclear blast could release dangerous chemical and biological agents which are normally kept in sealed containers in laboratories, factories, hospitals, and chemical plants. The deployment of chemical and biological weapons in stockpiles in Britain could also substantially increase this risk.

The total number of deaths to date resulting from the combined attacks on Hiroshima and Nagasaki amount to about 200,000 – about three times the initial casualties. For several reasons, however, it is not possible to make a direct comparison between the long-term fatalities resulting from the Japanese attacks and the fatalities resulting from the Square Leg nuclear attack on the UK. First, the Japanese bombs were air-bursts and of comparatively small yield (13 and 22 kilotons) by modern standards. Secondly, only two Japanese cities were devastated in this way, leaving many hospitals and rescue services unharmed elsewhere. Since ground-bursts were used on some Square Leg targets in the

---

Radiation and cancer

● Recent research links the occurrence of cancer to defects in the chromosomes inside human cells. Although many of the reasons for such chromosomal defects are not fully understood, one reason for them cannot be disputed. This is the effect of radiation.

Chromosomes consist of a large number of genes which carry information about cell structure and which are made up of DNA molecules. Radioactive material trapped inside the body (or external to the body) emitting high energy alpha, beta, or gamma radiation can damage DNA molecules and so damage the chromosomes. When a cell replicates it divides and passes on a new set of chromosomes to its replica. The chromosomes in the new cell exactly mirror the chromosomes in the original cell and hence any genetic misinformation is passed on. In this way the number of cancerous cells in the body increases and malignant tumours can grow. The precise time taken for clinically diagnosable cancer to appear will depend very much on ambient radioactivity levels, on the amount of radioactive material accumulated inside the body, on its precise location, and on the extent to which it is damaging cell chromosomes. Symptoms may not appear for several years.

The principal evidence for the cancer-inducing effects of low-level radioactivity is that higher than normal incidences of cancer are found (over a period of a few decades) in populations which have been exposed to this radiation. Such evidence is readily available from Japan, where high incidences of various forms of cancer have been reported amongst the 'Hibakusha' — the survivors of Hiroshima and Nagasaki.

UK, many more people would have accumulated small to medium doses of radiation (10–100 rads) than they did in Japan. But in the UK the breakdown of public services and health care would have caused many more people to die in the first few months than in the longer term.

☐ Damage to the atmosphere

Another possibly serious consequence of nuclear war apart from radiation could be the loss of the Earth's atmospheric ozone layer which protects us from dangerous rays from the sun.

The atmosphere which surrounds the Earth consists of about four-fifths nitrogen and one-fifth oxygen with small amounts of water vapour, carbon dioxide, ozone, and a few other trace gases. Several of these atmospheric constituents are absolutely vital for life to exist on the surface of the planet. The most obvious examples are oxygen, essential for human and animal life, and carbon dioxide, which is essential for plants. Ozone, although it has a very low concentration in the atmosphere (a few parts per million, most of which is found in the stratosphere at an altitude of 12–20 miles), is also vital for life on Earth because it absorbs ultraviolet rays from the sun. Long exposure to ultraviolet radiation can cause both skin cancers and retinal damage to the eye, so an ultraviolet shield is essential. Damage to the ozone layer would affect the amount of solar energy absorbed into the atmosphere and could therefore cause severe climatic changes. Some scientists believe that a nuclear war could significantly reduce the amount of ozone in the atmosphere and so destroy this shield – a serious threat to long-term survival for many forms of life. But how might this happen? To answer this question we must look at the various factors controlling the production and destruction of ozone in the stratosphere. If more ozone is being destroyed than is being created then the total amount of ozone in the atmosphere will decrease. When air is heated above a temperature of about 2,,000 °C, as in the fire-ball of a nuclear explosion, large quantities of nitrogen oxides are produced through the combination of nitrogen and oxygen. The addition of large quantities of such oxides can boost substantially the overall rate of destruction of ozone since they play a key role in some of the reactions which destroy it.

The hypothesis is therefore quite simple: the amount of nitrogen oxides generated by all the nuclear explosions in a war would be sufficiently large to destroy most of the ozone. But this hypothesis is very difficult to prove because the chemistry of ozone creation and destruction is not fully understood. There is no firm consensus among scientists about the atmospheric effects of nuclear war.[39] However, a recent analysis of observational evidence suggests that the concentration of ozone in the atmosphere was indeed reduced by a few per cent after nuclear testing in the early 1960s.[40] If this reduction was in fact caused entirely by a

---

Ozone chemistry

● Under normal conditions the oxygen in the atmosphere consists primarily of 'molecular oxygen' – this is in the form of two oxygen atoms joined together to form one molecule. This is the most abundant form of oxygen which we breathe. Under the influence of sunlight, however, some of these oxygen molecules split up (the process being known as photo-dissociation) to produce two individual oxygen atoms. These oxygen atoms may then recombine to form molecular oxygen or one of them may join on to an existing oxygen molecule to form ozone, which consists of three oxygen atoms joined together as a single molecule. These ozone molecules may subsequently split up to form atomic and molecular oxygen. Nitrogen oxides (and some other trace gases in the atmosphere) play vital roles in these chemical processes. The net amount of ozone existing in the atmosphere at any one time depends on the careful balance between creation and destruction and is to a large extent controlled by the concentrations of trace gases.

---

few nuclear test explosions, then those who survive the immediate effects of a nuclear war may have rather more to worry about in the long term than just the biological effects of fall-out. Exposure to daylight would become extremely dangerous and survivors would have to become nocturnal creatures. Other life-forms would be affected and it could mean the extinction of many species.

□ Summary

- Delayed fall-out can be carried round the globe far from the war zone.

- Exposure to low doses of radiation from both immediate and delayed fall-out causes higher cancer incidence amongst long-term survivors.

- Radiation damage to genes can cause babies to be born deformed.

- The ozone layer in the atmosphere could be destroyed by a large-scale nuclear conflict so that ultraviolet radiation from the sun could kill many forms of life.

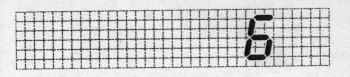

Civil Defence
and
Home Office
Policy

The last two years have seen something of a revival of the idea of civil defence against a nuclear attack on Britain. Indeed it was partly in response to official publicity that this book was produced. In this chapter we assess current Home Office plans for civil defence, discuss their likely role in a nuclear attack, and ask whether there is a viable alternative.

Civil defence in the Second World War was clearly very useful: the ARP, AFS, WRVS (Air Raid Patrol, Auxiliary Fire Service, Womens Royal Voluntary Service), and other organisations played a vital role in reducing casualties and maintaining morale. But whereas fewer than 20,000 people died in London during the Blitz,[41] *5 million* died in our simulation of a nuclear attack on London. The effective role of civil defence in these extreme conditions is an entirely different matter. Rescuing any reasonable proportion of survivors, for instance, which was the main role of the ARP in 1941, would be impossible because of high radiation levels, fires, and the vast numbers of buried people. Blitz experience showed that on average a party of eight rescuers can dig out two and a half people in an eight-hour shift: one million trapped would require over a million rescuers working one shift on and one off for 48 hours.[42] Home Office policy on civil defence has also changed drastically since the Second World War – the Civil Defence Corps, the direct descendent of the ARP, comprising 380,000 volunteers, was finally abolished in 1968. We need to examine carefully plans for civil defence against a nuclear attack, and to bear in mind that there is probably no analogy with previous experience of civil defence against conventional bombing.

□ Government and civil defence

According to Home Office plans, the structure of government following a nuclear attack would be as below:

National Seat of Government
|
12 Regional Seats of Government
|
23 Sub-Regional Headquarters
|
County Controls
|
District Controls
|
Sub-District Controls
|
Community Posts or Rest Centres

At the bottom are the Community Posts, located mainly in schools and colleges, staffed mainly by volunteers, and dealing directly with the population at large. Sub-District, District, and County Controls, and Sub-Regional Headquarters would be located in various sheltered sites, staffed by local authority civil servants.

National government would be dispersed in several secret bunkers, one of the most important being the UK Land

Forces Head Quarters (the army command). An idea of how the system would actually be run is given by General Sir John Hackett (former Deputy Chief of the General Staff and Commander of the Northern Army Group of NATO) and others in their book *The Third World War*. After the first attack, they say, 'delegation of power over military *and civil defence* resources had become the responsibility of the Head Quarters of the UK Land Forces' (p. 389, our emphasis). So these military authorities at least believe that the army would be in control of 'civil' defence nationally.

What would happen to regional government? Here there seems an inconsistency. An internal circular states that 'as soon as practicable, regional government would be established at a location in each region which offered the best surviving communications and accommodation'.[43] In the meantime, 'sub-regional Headquarters would be the highest effective level of internal government'. This means that there are no bunkers for civilian regional government and it is unclear where the Regional Commissioners and their staff would be stationed. What is not stated, however, is that there is one Armed Forces Headquarters per region, in a deep bunker containing the regional military commander and his staff. These would provide a higher 'effective level' of government – and it seems most likely that civilian regional government will be stationed in these *military* bunkers with minimal staff. Indeed, there is extensive evidence of a chain of heavily protected bunkers and buildings from which the government will operate after an attack.[42,44]

This is consistent with the purpose of the new civil defence measures as defined in internal Home Office circular ES3/73 sent to local authorities: 'The current aims of home defence are defined as those defensive measures necessary in the United Kingdom . . . to secure the United Kingdom against any internal threat.'[45] Civil defence has now, it seems, become a matter of not only protecting survivors from the effects of nuclear war but also protecting government from survivors (Civil Defence includes Home Defence and Emergency Planning).

The role of civil defence would be similar at sub-regional level. Staff of Sub-Regional Headquarters 'would aim at the conservation of resources ... for longer-term survival – rather than immediate short-term aid to the hardest hit areas. Sub-Regional Commissioners would be concerned with : ... the maintenance by the police of law and order and with the general behaviour and morale of the survivors.'[43] From our calculations the 'hardest hit areas' would probably include all of London.

Local authority civil servants and civil defence volunteers would find that their main role was to control survivors and preserve a military-controlled government. The Government has certainly not made this aspect of civil defence clear to the general public.

□ The civil defence revival

So what is the nature of the civil defence revival? It has two aspects: the publicity and the preparations.

Publicity

Recent publicity is aimed at promoting the idea of *individual* survival. You are supposed to build or buy your own shelter and to stay at home before, during, and after the attack. The help given by government towards your survival will be negligible: there will be no public shelters, no evacuation of cities, and no public services for some time after the attack. Moreover, we have found (pp.44–8) that the 'do-it-yourself' civil defence measures as outlined by the Home Office are severely inadequate.

Worse still are the semi-official unpublished estimates of the likely effects of a nuclear attack on Britain. An example is the 'official' estimate quoted by John Clayton, Director of the Home Office Scientific Advisory Branch,[46] that 75 per cent of the population of Britain would be alive twelve months after an attack of similar size to Square Leg (about 200 megatons) if everyone followed Home Office advice. In our 'attack' 5 million people out of a population of 7 million died in Greater London alone in the first few months, killed by just six bombs totalling 13 megatons in and around the Greater London area. That is roughly 10 per cent of the population of Britain. In Square Leg, 187 megatons (119 bombs) fell elsewhere, many being direct hits on large cities. Considering the casualties produced by just six bombs this 'official' estimate appears to be rather optimistic. For example, a recent independent study showed that just 50 one-megaton bombs dropped over major population centres could kill half the population of the UK by blast alone.[47]

Preparations

Increasing pressure has been applied on local authorities to prepare War Plans, to set up wartime headquarters, to appoint and train staff to carry out the plans, and to recruit and train volunteers to run the community posts.[18] There has been an increase in training facilities for staff and volunteers (mainly Red Cross, WRVS, etc.) at the Home Defence College at Easingwold. The UK Warning and Monitoring Organisation is being modernised. The Government is also spending £23 million a year on constructing deep shelters from which to govern. Expenditure on civil defence has been increased from £27 million a year to £45 million a year.[19]

These preparations, however, have been plagued with difficulties. There is widespread lack of confidence in Home Office advice and more than 100 local authorities of all political complexions have refused to co-operate (see Figure 16).

Tory-controlled Huntingdon Council (which has the proposed cruise missile site at Molesworth on its territory) passed in 1980 a 'non co-operation' motion, and later a motion declaring that the present civil defence provision

Fig. 16 Local authorities opposed to Government nuclear and civil defence policies (listed opposite)

was 'absurd' and calling on the Government to provide money for public shelters.[44] The Labour-controlled Haringey Council declared in 1980:

This council believes that it is important for the people of Haringey to know that it will be impossible to provide adequate protection for them in the event of a nuclear attack, and declares that it will not be party to civil defence exercise[s] designed to mislead the public into believing that adequate protection is

Adur	Forest of Dean	North West
Afan	Gateshead	Leicestershire
Allerdale	Glamorgan	North West
Barnsley	Glasgow	Derbyshire
Barrow in	Glyndwr	Norwich
Furness	Greenwich	Ogwr
Blackburn	Greater London	Oxford
Blaenau Gwent	Gwent	Pendle
Blyth Valley	Gwynedd	Powys
Brecknock	Hackney	Preston
Brent	Haringey	Rochdale
Bristol	Harlow	Rotherham
Burnley	Hatfield	Salop
Bury	Hereford	Sandwell
Cambridge	Huntingdon	Scunthorpe
Camden	Hydeburn	Sedgefield
Carlisle	Islington	Sheffield
Chesterfield	Islwyn	South Bucks
Chester-le-	Kingston-	South Tyneside
Street	upon-Hull	South Yorks
Clwyd	Kirklees	St Helens
Clydebank	Knowlsey	Stoke on Trent
Corby	Langbaurgh	Strathclyde
Coventry	Leeds	Tameside
Crawley	Leicester	Torfaen
Crewe and	Lewisham	Tower Hamlets
Nantwich	Liverpool	Tyne and Wear
Darlington	Lynysmon	Walsall
Derby	Malvern Hills	Watford
Derwentside	Manchester	Wear Valley
Desborough	Merham	Welwyn
Dinefwr	Merseyside	Western Isles
Doncaster	Newcastle	Wolverhampton
Durham Co.	upon Tyne	Worcester
Dwyfor	Newham	Worthing
Dyfed	Newport	Wrekin
		Wrexham Maelor

available and therefore that 'limited' nuclear war and increased military spending are acceptable.[48]

Many District Councils (such as Islington and Watford) have made their War Plans publicly available as a means of demonstrating their inadequacy and the impossible position councils would be in if faced with a nuclear attack. We believe that those councils which have expressed disquiet at these plans are fully justified in doing so. So it is necessary to ask: What is the alternative? Should the Government be spending money on public shelters or evacuation? Is there any effective civil defence against nuclear war?

Before attempting to answer these questions we have to deal with the more fundamental questions underlying the problem: What is the risk of a nuclear attack on Britain? And how large might that attack be?

☐ The risk of nuclear war in the UK

Target Britain

As the map in Figure 17 shows, Britain is very liberally sprinked with targets of one sort or another, such as: American and British nuclear submarine bases at Holy Loch and Faslane; nuclear weapons based by the US Air Force (USAF) and RAF in airfields around the country; major US and NATO communication centres; bases for receiving and maintaining North American reinforcements should war break out in Europe; and industrial and economic centres which would be disabled to prevent them posing any threat after a war.

Current Government plans are to expand the present nuclear arsenal by buying American Trident submarine-launched missiles. They also plan to allow ground-launched cruise missiles under US control to be based at Greenham Common and Molesworth, and to be widely dispersed over the countryside in times of tension.

Considering the number and importance of the military

◆ Communications/
  surveillance centre

★ Nuclear submarine base
  (Holy Loch and Faslane)

O US base

▽ Weapons store

● RAF/Fleet air arm

+ Naval base

▲ Major military command
  centre

▲ Nuclear power station /
  reprocessing facility

A Aldermaston

B Porton Down

C Molesworth and
  Greenham Common
  (proposed cruise
  missile bases)

Fig. 17 Target Britain

bases in this country there can be no doubt that the UK would be a prime target in the event of nuclear war.

In order for an attacker to be sure of eliminating all these targets the weapons used would far exceed the 200 megatons of the Square Leg exercise. Indeed, as stated in Chapter 3, the Government estimates that an attack of over 1,000 megatons would be needed to destroy the cruise missiles alone.

□ Alternative civil defence measures

Public shelter option

Neutral countries such as Switzerland and Sweden which have no nuclear missiles on their soil, may not be certain targets. Their public shelters are intended to offer protection against fall-out created from nuclear war occurring on battlefields outside their national boundaries. When danger from fall-out has passed, their own economic structure would be essentially intact. Serious economic and social disruption would still occur, but the scale of destruction and desolation would not be anything like that experienced in the Square Leg exercise.

The Home Office view is that to provide fall-out shelters for everybody would be too expensive – between £60,000 and £80,000 million at 1980 prices,[46] which is roughly £1,000 to £1,500 per head of population. At present, expenditure on civil defence amounts to about 50–85 pence per head of population. But even if the Government were prepared to bear the cost, would a UK public shelter programme be effective? As long as the UK maintains its present level of nuclear arms, its commitment to current NATO policy, its UK-sited key NATO and USA bases, it will remain a certain target. In the event of a nuclear attack on a scale that NATO thinks likely, such shelters would increase the number of short-term survivors, only for them to face the appalling medium- and long-term problems of the aftermath already described in Chapter 4.

It is possible that an attack might occur by surprise or by accident. In this case there would be as little as a few minutes warning during which time very few people would be able to reach the shelters.

There is no guarantee that a nuclear attack would be over quickly. It may be spread over a period of several weeks or even longer. The time spent in deep shelters would then be very prolonged. In this case the further strain on resources, food, and water, and the effect of increased stress on survivors would be magnified beyond all current estimates.

We must conclude that public shelters are not a realistic option for this country.

Evacuation policy

Protect and Survive says, 'No part of the United Kingdom can be considered safe from both the direct effects of the weapons and the resultant fall-out.'[14] For that reason, it suggests, evacuation is not a sensible policy. However, it is certainly true that important cities and military bases are more likely to be targets than is the open countryside. The entrepreneurs who are building Community Nuclear Survival Units for those who can afford the necessary £10,000 or so, are siting them in the remotest countryside they can find.

Protect and Survive also says, 'If you move away – unless you have a place of your own to go to or intend to live with relatives – the authority in your new area will not help you with accommodation or food or other essentials.'[14] There are many reasons why evacuation would not be a sensible policy.

● The problems of organising an evacuation and arranging for the reception of the evacuees are enormous, and the consequent economic dislocation severe.

● Evacuation is not possible without sufficient warning of attack.

● If the Government did put an evacuation into motion it would necessarily take several days to carry through. An adversary could interpret the evacuation as a preparation for war on our part. Simply by increasing the scale of attack, an opponent could still kill as many people as if evacuation had not occurred.

☐ The breakdown of 'deterrence'

The Home Office position on civil defence against nuclear attack is based on the idea that nuclear weapons are a deterrent. These weapons are supposed to prevent the Russians launching an attack on us for fear of massive retaliation. It is argued that nuclear deterrence has kept the peace in Europe since the Second World War. The 'deterrence' works both ways (each side faces massive retaliation if it attacks first) and is sometimes called Mutually Assured Destruction or MAD. Since we need nuclear weapons to keep the peace, the argument runs, we must learn to live with the threat of their eventual use. That is why we need civil defence against a nuclear attack.

We have shown that there is no effective civil defence against a nuclear attack. This being so, our only remaining defence is to prevent such an attack ever occurring. We therefore ask: Is it true that nuclear weapons protect us against nuclear war? Or might they in fact be the cause of nuclear war?

The weapons

The position of mutual deterrence is continually undermined by the production and technological advance of nuclear weapons on both sides.

The newer missiles have vastly increased accuracies due to the development of terminal guidance systems. The Pershing II missile, for instance, is accurate to around 45 metres. The advances in technology have now reached the point where these missiles are capable of destroying an opponent's missiles in their silos. Such high accuracy is only useful in a 'first strike' – a surprise attack aimed at destroying almost all the opponent's missiles. For there is no point in attacking silos from which the missiles have already been fired. This accuracy is also far greater than that needed for 'deterrence', which only requires the threat of the destruction of large cities and industrial sites. A nuclear weapons policy which is at the same time potentially offensive ('first strike') and defensive ('deterrent') is in deep contradiction. An enemy who cannot distinguish whether the intent is offensive or defensive must assume the worst – that it is in constant danger of an attack in which its own missiles would be destroyed. This may soon lead to the adoption of a 'Launch on Warning' policy on both sides. In addition, the speed of modern weapons – Pershing II could reach Moscow from Germany in less than ten minutes – means there would be little time to assess the scale of an attack. 'Launch on Warning' would have to be controlled largely by computers in order to respond quickly enough. But all computers have one characteristic in common – they fail. In 1980 it was reported that

Three times in less than a year NORAD (North American Air Defence Command) computers have detected a nuclear attack which was not actually taking place. On each occasion the crews of B52 nuclear bombers raced to their aircraft for take-off and the crews [sic] of intercontinental missiles began preliminary launch procedures.[49]

Technological advance has thus greatly increased the threat of a nuclear war starting by accident.

The numbers of nuclear weapons are increasing rapidly. Between 1970 and 1980, the number of large, 'strategic' nuclear warheads trebled on both sides. They now stand at around 9,000 for the USA and 6,000 for the USSR.[50] Considering the destruction that six of these caused in London in our study, these numbers are obviously vastly in excess of what is needed to inflict massive devastation on either side – much more than is needed for 'deterrence'. The large numbers of weapons also require increasingly complex systems for their control, with a consequent increased risk of nuclear war starting by accident.

The strategies

The strategy of 'deterrence' has been a very difficult one to maintain. A recent official report to the Committee on Foreign Affairs in the US Congress opened,

For over two decades NATO's theatre nuclear strategy has been *the* source of controversy and strain within the alliance. These tensions have been based in large part on differing perceptions in the United States and in Europe concerning whether theatre nuclear weapons are principally to serve as tools of deterrence or as instruments of a *war-fighting capacity*[51] [our emphasis].

A compromise seems to have been struck in the strategy of 'flexible response', the official NATO strategy and the one outlined in Ministry of Defence publications. It means that whatever level of attack NATO is faced with, whether conventional or nuclear, it will reply with whatever force necessary to 'deter' further attack. This means *using* weapons at a higher level than those used in the original attack in order to threaten further destruction should that attack continue. The assumption is that if war has broken out at one level it can be contained by 'deterrence', i.e. use of weapons, at the next level. This strategy is used to justify the deployment of a full spectrum of nuclear weapons (see Appendix 6), each type to be used at a particular stage of escalation. For instance, a 'conventional' attack with tanks would be met with 'battlefield' nuclear shells and neutron bombs. If these brought a similar reply, medium-range weapons such as cruise missiles or nuclear bombers would be used. Finally, if none of these stopped the war, the larger 'strategic' weapons would be used to destroy the opponent completely.

It is hardly credible that this strategy would ever work.

Each side would have to withold using larger weapons and risk their possible destruction before they were used. Even if commanders were able to keep detailed control of their forces there would probably be a staged escalation culminating in full-scale nuclear war. Far more likely, military communications would be disrupted at an early stage, at which point local commanders would let fly with all the weapons at their disposal.

The crucial point, however, is that NATO strategy involves the possible 'first use' by NATO of 'tactical' nuclear weapons in response to a conventional, i.e. non-nuclear, attack. These smaller (although still immensely destructive) weapons have thus lowered the nuclear 'threshold' and made more possible the initiation of nuclear war (see Notes 17 and 51 for discussion and details).

Further, a nuclear war waged in Europe ('theatre' nuclear war) would in all likelihood quickly spread to become an all-out war waged between the mainland US and USSR. This has been stated by a number of military authorities:

It is not a concept which any sensible responsible military person now holds that you would fight a war in Europe with tactical or theatre nuclear weapons and thus avoid a strategic nuclear exchange.[52]

> Lord Carver (the former Chief of Defence Staff)

the belief that nuclear weapons . . . could be used in field warfare without triggering an all-out nuclear exchange leading to the final holocaust is more and more incredible.[53]

> Lord Mountbatten

I do not think it at all likely that a limited nuclear exchange would remain limited.[54]

> Harold Brown (US Secretary of Defence in the Carter administration)

☐ The alternative

The arguments above suggest that the strategy of deterrence has broken down.

What is the alternative? We believe that there is only one way out: positive and immediate action to reduce the risk of nuclear war. The real question is not, Do we need nuclear weapons? but, How can we get rid of them? The main priorities for achieving a reduction in weapons are:

● a halt to further research, development, and production of nuclear weapons
● decisions against any further deployment of nuclear weapons
● the planned dismantling of existing nuclear weapons systems.

The mechanisms for achieving the rational reduction and dismantling of nuclear weapons are complex and deserve careful study which is outside the scope of this book. Nevertheless it is imperative to explore these mechanisms. Above all, new ways of keeping the peace between East and West must be found. We cannot rely on 'deterrence' any longer.

☐ Summary

● Civil defence along the lines of the Second World War organisations would be totally inadequate in a nuclear war.

● After a nuclear attack the country would to a large extent be run by the military or civil servants and not by an elected government.

● Civil defence would be concerned not only with protecting survivors from the effects of nuclear war, but also with protecting the Government against the survivors.

● The actual help that central government could give towards the survival of ordinary members of the public under nuclear attack would be negligible.

● The Home Office plans for civil defence, including its

shelter policy and non-evacuation policy, combine to reinforce the notion that nuclear war is survivable, thinkable, and that casualties could be kept at 'acceptable' levels. The Home Office civil defence policy, by underestimating the devastating reality of nuclear war, reduces public pressure on the Government to reduce the risks of nuclear war.

● There can be *no* effective civil defence against an all-out nuclear attack.

● Technological advances in weapon systems have greatly increased the threat of a nuclear war starting by accident.

● The breakdown of the strategy of deterrence has brought us closer to nuclear war.

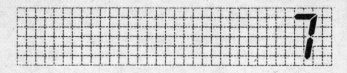

Conclusions

The consequences of a nuclear conflict would be so devastating that there could be no adequate protection for a population against the immediate effects of blast, fire, and radiation or against the long-term damage caused to the Earth's natural environment. This is the overwhelming conclusion of our study. Even in our analysis of a nuclear attack in which only four warheads explode in the Greater London area and two nearby, there would be destruction and loss of life on a scale never seen before.

The facts are these: immediately after the attack 16 per cent of London's population would be dead; another 60 per cent would die over the next 6–12 weeks from radiation sickness, leaving 7 per cent injured and 17 per cent un-injured. Medical care for these survivors would be virtually non-existent and the biological effects of delayed fall-out, environmental damage, and the destruction of public services would combine to make survival questionable for years ahead; even babies born years after the event might suffer severe genetic damage.

Although 12 weeks after the attack 76 per cent of the Greater London population (amounting to over 5 million people) would be dead, only 16 per cent would actually die during the attack. The remainder could live on for weeks without medical care, dying slowly of multiple injuries or radiation sickness. They would huddle together in primitive shelters with little food or water, no sanitary facilities, no heating, no lighting, and no protection from the weather. They would suffer from diarrhoea and vomiting, would lose their hair, and suffer severe psychological distress. They would see members of their own family die slowly and painfully without any relief. They would not know if they themselves were about to die. If they ventured outside they would see a charred blackened landscape, heaps of rubble, and decomposing bodies. Life would be a nightmare and the living might well envy the dead.

This extremely grim picture emerged from our study even assuming the most favourable conditions for survival. First, when we consider that there are now about 40,000 nuclear warheads in the world, and that London is the capital of one of the major nuclear powers, it seems hardly credible that in the event of a genuine attack only six warheads would be targeted on the London area and none on Inner London. Secondly, we assumed that the attack followed the Square Leg simulation precisely and that there was a period of four days between the declaration of war and the onset of the nuclear attack, giving time for preparations. More importantly, we assumed that everyone built their own *Protect and Survive* shelters at home as the Home Office would have advised them to do. In reality, there might be only a few minutes warning of an attack and no time to go home to stock up with food and water, and build a shelter.

The picture which we have painted differs considerably from that put forward publicly by the Home Office. To be specific, the Home Office:

- underestimates the extent of blast damage
- underestimates blast casualities
- overestimates the protection ordinary housing gives against radiation
- omits to consider the very important effect of blast damage in reducing protection against radiation
- glosses over most of the extreme difficulties that would face survivors in the weeks and years after attack.

As a result of these omissions and inaccuracies, anyone

calculating total casualty figures on the basis of publicised Home Office information would arrive at estimates which would be much too low.

Clearly the Home Office is fully aware of the terrible consequences of nuclear war. Indeed in their internal circulars quoted throughout this book they describe in some detail the true scale of devastation, and their plans for running the country afterwards. But *Protect and Survive* and *Domestic Nuclear Shelters* completely ignore the very important topics raised in the internal circulars.

Why do the Home Office pamphlets available to the public so severely underestimate the effects of nuclear attack? Why do these pamphlets ignore the issues raised in the internal circulars? These are vitally important questions which require answers from the Home Office. Whatever the reasons, the effect is that the Home Office is making nuclear war appear more survivable than it really would be. The danger is that civil defence is made to look more effective than it ever could be and that people begin to believe that they could survive a nuclear war. This increasingly vigorous promotion of civil defence comes at a time when we are being asked to accept the siting of American ground-launched cruise missiles on our soil and are about to buy the American Trident missile system at enormous cost to the country.

We have considered various conventional civil defence options and shown that there is no adequate civil defence against nuclear attack. In particular, the measures advised by the Home Office would be totally inadequate for most of the population, and the widespread opposition of many local authorities to current civil defence plans is in our view completely justified. This is not to say that *all* civil defence measures are completely useless – indeed they might prolong the lives of a few people. However, any such measures would be inadequate for most people, and should never be presented otherwise.

We conclude that there is *only one* worthwhile form of

civil defence – *positive* action to reduce the risk of nuclear war. Present policies for the further deployment of increasingly sophisticated nuclear weapons only make war more likely. These policies must be reversed if the ultimate catastrophe is to be avoided.

Appendix
1

Scaling laws for calculating blast

The sizes of the blast rings from a one-megaton ground-burst and a one-megaton air-burst at 6,000 feet are shown in Figure 18. The blast rings in the air-burst explosion extend further because a more powerful shock-wave is formed from the combination of the blast from the explosion and that reflected from the ground. The sizes of the blast rings from a bomb of different size are proportional to the cube root of the explosive power of the bomb. Taking the example of a 5-megaton ground-burst, the blast radii would all extend $\sqrt[3]{5}$ or 1.7 times further than for a one-megaton ground-burst. For an air-burst the situation is a little more complicated because the height of the burst should also be scaled in the same way. Taking

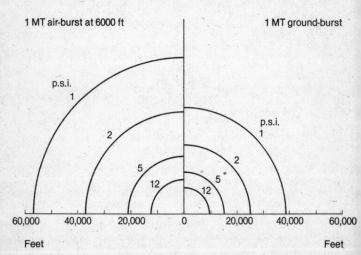

1 MT air-burst at 6000 ft   1 MT ground-burst

p.s.i.
1
2
5
12

p.s.i.
1
2
5
12

| 60,000 | 40,000 | 20,000 | 0 | 20,000 | 40,000 | 60,000 |

Feet   Feet

Fig. 18 Extent of blast from an air-burst and a ground-burst

another example, that of a 100,000-ton ($\frac{1}{10}$-megaton) air-burst, the new blast radii would be reduced by a factor of $\sqrt[3]{1/10}$ or 0.46. The altitude of explosion for which these radii apply would now be $6,000 \times 0.46 = 2670$ feet.

For further details see Glasstone and Dolan (eds.), *The Effects of Nuclear Weapons*.

Appendix 2

Radiation from fall-out

This appendix describes how we calculated the spread of fall-out resulting from ground-bursts of one-, two-, and three-megaton nuclear weapons as detonated in Operation Square Leg. These calculations were closely based upon methods and data provided by the US Department of Defense and Department of Energy in *The Effects of Nuclear Weapons* edited by Glasstone and Dolan (we will refer to this as 'G & D' for short).

Basic assumptions

The method we have used results in an 'idealised fall-out plume' in which fall-out is spread in a quite regular cigar-shaped (elliptical) pattern downwind of the explosion. As one might expect, in reality fall-out is not spread by the wind in such a simply predictable way. But in order to make any calculation some simplifying assumptions have to be made. The assumptions were made following G & D:

- The wind velocity is a steady 15 m.p.h.
- The density of air is constant and the humidity typical of a temperate zone.
- The radioactive dust cloud expands to its maximum radius above ground zero before appreciable fall-out from the cloud reaches the ground.
- The terrain is flat (although the roughness of the ground is taken into account).

Other factors which are not taken into account because of their complex and unpredictable nature are: changes in wind direction, differences in wind directions at different altitudes, turbulence, fall-out brought down by rain, and the effect of land relief. Effects such as these can produce quite an irregular spread of fall-out or the occurrence of 'hot spots' of radiation as shown in Figure 5.

However, the overriding justification for using the simplifying assumptions is that although the spread of fall-out may not be found exactly as predicted, the calculations do predict an average distribution of fall-out in which any overestimates and under-estimates tend to cancel out. This method is therefore valid for calculating the numbers of people affected by radiation, provided that the population is distributed fairly evenly.

Details of the calculation procedure

The calculation is divided into two main sections:

● the calculation of the Unit Time Reference Dose Rate (UDR)
● calculation of the accumulated dose

After the fall-out has been deposited, the approximate dose rate is given by UDR × $t^{-1.2}$ where t is the time after the explosion. The UDR is used to calculate dose rates at any time after the explosion and to calculate the dose accumulated over a period of time after the explosion.

Contours of UDR were drawn for bombs of one, two, and three megatons assuming a steady 15 m.p.h. wind. Data supplied in G & D Table 9.93 were rescaled by a factor of 0.35 to account for a fission yield of 50 per cent and a surface roughness factor of 0.7.

The accumulated dose was calculated in two parts:

● the dose accumulated after all the fall-out has been deposited (after the cloud has passed overhead)
● the dose accumulated as the cloud passes overhead and while fall-out is still being deposited.

Both parts of the calculation require a knowledge of the size of the cloud. From G & D Figure 2.16 the cloud radii for the one-, two-, and three-megaton bombs are given as 6, 7.5, and 9.5 miles respectively. It was assumed that the clouds drift downwind at 15 m.p.h.

● This accumulated dose is obtained by multiplying UDR by a factor dependent upon the time period before fall-out arrives (entry time) and the time over which radiation is received. This factor was obtained from G & D Figure 9.26 using an entry time calculated for each cloud and a completion time of two weeks.
● It was assumed that the cloud had a uniform distribution of

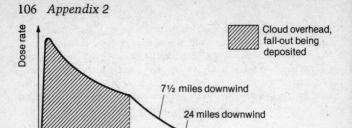

Fig. 19 Radiation dose rate downwind of a 2MT ground-burst

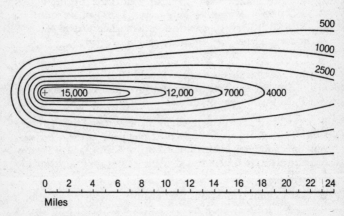

Fig. 20 Accumulated radiation dose (rads) after 2 weeks for a 1 MT ground-burst

fall-out and that fall-out was deposited at a uniform rate. At each stage of the cloud's arrival, the dose rate was estimated from G & D Figure 9.16a and corrected by multiplying by the fraction of the fall-out that had arrived at that time. For example, after 25 per cent of the fall-out has arrived the dose rate is a quarter of what it would be otherwise. As a result the radiation levels reach a peak as more fall-out is deposited and then gradually fall off as the radioactivity decays (see Figure 19). The total dose received as the cloud passes is given by the shaded area under the left-hand side of the curves. This dose is then added to the dose received over the remaining period (right-hand side of the curves), giving the total accumulation dose over two weeks.

Because of lack of space, we cannot include all the detailed UDR and two-week accumulated dose contours that were drawn, but as an example, Figure 20 shows the accumulated dose for a one-megaton ground-burst.

Appendix 3

Protection against radiation

Home Office protection factors

The protection offered by a building to its occupants against radiation from nuclear fall-out depends on many factors such as:

- the size of the building
- the thickness and weight of the walls
- the size and location of openings (windows, doors, cracks, etc.).

The protection factor (PF) can be defined by the equation $PF = 100 \div r$, where r is the dose rate received inside a building expressed as a percentage of the open-air unshielded dose rate. The protection factor is extremely difficult to calculate accurately and varies from building to building and also from one spot to another inside the same building. The Home Office publication *Nuclear Weapons* gives approximate protection factors for several types of dwellings calculated with the rather unlikely assumption that doors and windows are blocked up with material of the same weight and thickness as the surrounding walls.[23] Similar figures are given in another recent Home Office publication, *Domestic Nuclear Shelters: Technical Guidance*.

In *Domestic Nuclear Shelters: Technical Guidance* an example PF calculation is given for an end-of-terrace house with unobstructed windows and doors.[11] A PF of 10 is derived, which is, as would be expected, much lower than for a house with bricked-up windows and doors. As one side of this building is protected by the terrace row, the protection factor is higher than for a detached house but lower than for a mid-terrace house or a flat in the middle of a block.

The Home Office make a number of assumptions in their calculations. In particular it is assumed that:

- Fall-out is deposited uniformly on the ground and on the roof.

- There is no fall-out deposited on the walls, window sills, or other projections from the building.
- No fall-out enters the building.

The first two assumptions are incorrect because fall-out, just like other airborne particles such as dust and sand, does not settle uniformly but piles up against walls, in cracks and crevices, and particularly on window sills and guttering. The third assumption is invalid because, even in the absence of blast damage, fall-out particles will enter a house unless it is completely airtight. It is difficult to correct these assumptions because of the uncertainties involved, but certainly they all combine to reduce the protection factor. Fall-out deposited on window sills or against doors is particularly important in reducing the protection factor because it is a source of radiation just by the thinnest parts of the outside walls.

In addition to these assumptions, the Home Office make an approximation in their calculations which leads to a further overestimation of the protection factor. Variations in the thickness of walls, floors, and roof are averaged over their total area. In their calculation for the end-of-terrace house, the thickness of one of the external walls with 30 per cent window area has been calculated by averaging the thickness of solid wall over the entire window and wall area. This is incorrect because, for the wall in question, the radiation getting through the window has been underestimated by 'spreading' the wall thickness over the window in the averaging process. This point also applies to the averaged figure the Home Office use for the weight of a wall or roof without apertures. A roof, for example, is made up of heavier and lighter parts, and taking the average weight has the effect of 'spreading' the heavier parts over the entire roof.

Protection factors for our assessment of Square Leg

For a simulated nuclear attack such as Square Leg it is necessary to use realistic protection factors to estimate casualties from fall-out. In our assessment of the attack (Chapter 3) it is assumed that all householders in London are able to follow the advice given in *Protect and Survive*. To be more specific, it is assumed that everyone builds an 'inner refuge' out of boards, books, sand-bags, etc. inside their 'fall-out room'. We also assume that householders do not have sufficient materials or time to brick-up their doors and windows. It would certainly not be possible for every home in London to acquire about 3,000 bricks hastily in the pre-attack period.

To estimate fall-out casualties reliably, the protection factor for dwellings must be estimated *after* the blast has done its damage. In general an inner refuge would improve the protection of a house but only if it remained undamaged. According to *Domestic Nuclear Shelters: Technical Guidance*, however, Type 1 improvised shelters (such as suggested in *Protect and Survive*) can only withstand blast pressures of up to 1.5 p.s.i.[11] Our analysis of Square Leg shows that three-quarters of the GLC area is subjected to a blast pressure of at least 2 p.s.i. Hence the majority of Type 1 shelters in London collapse, leaving only the fabric of the building to offer fall-out protection. Ironically, the only inner refuge shelters remaining are located mainly in the East End of London, where radiation levels are lowest anyway.

The PF value for a typical London home will depend on the extent of blast damage it receives. Different PF values must therefore be used for different blast zones. The most appropriate Home Office PF value to use for the Square Leg attack is the value 10 given for the house with unblocked windows. Bearing in mind the incorrect assumption involved in its derivation, this value must be regarded as an upper limit even in areas with *no* blast damage. But in Square Leg, windows are smashed throughout the GLC area and corrections must be made for fall-out which enters buildings and acts as an unshielded source of radiation.

It is impossible to predict accurately how much fall-out dust would enter a damaged building. It is, however, reasonable to expect that the ratio (which we refer to as r_i) of the dose rate received inside the building from internal fall-out to the open-air unshielded dose rate, is roughly related to the ratio of apertures in the building (i.e. blown-in doors and windows, missing roof tiles, etc.) to the total outside wall and roof area. Expressing r_i as a percentage, we therefore assume that:

$$r_i = 100 \times \frac{\text{area of apertures}}{\text{total area of roof and outside walls}} \qquad \text{Eqn. 1}$$

The protection factor for a blast-damaged building can now be worked out by considering the percentage contributions from radiation outside and inside using the following equation:

Table 8 Estimated protection factors for blast-damaged housing (London)

Blast-damage zones	r_i	Typical damage	PF range (calculated using Equation 3)	
			Lower limit	Upper limit
A	90 or more	Houses and flats completely destroyed	1	1
B	40–90	Most housing destroyed, walls blown down, roofs removed	1	2
C	10–40	Severe roof damage, walls cracked	2	5
D	2–10	Windows smashed, doors blown in, some roof tiles removed	5	10

Note: Although a range of values is given for r_i, the higher values are more likely to be found in practice. These values thus give a conservative range of protection factors to apply for blast-damaged housing, and were applied in our calculations of radiation casualties. Home Office protection factors above 10 are inappropriate for almost all London in the Square Leg simulation.

$$PF = \frac{100}{r_e + r_i} \qquad \text{Eqn. 2}$$

where r_e is the dose rate received inside the building from external fall-out as a percentage of the open-air unshielded dose rate. This protection factor can now be calculated once suitable values for r_e and r_i are put in the equation. Using the Home Office PF of 10 for an undamaged house we arrive at a conservative value of 10 per cent for r_e. On average, flats are somewhat more protective than houses because they shield one another, thus a value of 5 per cent for r_e is appropriate for flats. Both these figures result in overestimates of the PF values because they take no account of the increase of r_e due to blast damage. In London 30 per cent of the population live in purpose-built flats and 70 per cent in ordinary housing, so the overall protection factor taking into account both types of housing is given by:

$$PF_{average} = \frac{70}{10 + r_i \text{ (house)}} + \frac{30}{5 + r_i \text{ (flat)}} \qquad \text{Eqn. 3}$$

A range of values for r_i (because of apertures produced by blast) have to be estimated for each blast zone. The same range of r_i values have been used for houses and flats. The values of r_i used and the resulting protection factors applicable for London are given in Table 8.

Appendix 4

Calculation of casualties

This appendix describes the details of calculating casualties from blast and radiation, and factors affecting the level of burns casualties.

Blast casualties

The calculation method follows that of the US Office of Technology Assessment.

Given the explosive power of a specific bomb and whether it is an air-burst or a ground-burst, zones of blast pressure can be worked out after scaling distances up or down from a one-megaton bomb (see Appendix 1). For each bomb, rings of blast pressure at 12, 5, 2, and 1 p.s.i. are drawn on a map. These blast levels define the Zones A, B, C and D as used in Chapter 3 (see Table 4, p.36). The number of people in each zone are now counted. Census figures give the distribution of the night-time population. For the daytime population, allowances must be made for workers commuting into towns and cities. Once the numbers in each zone are known for the time of day of the explosion, blast casualties can be worked out from Table 9. These casualty percentages apply to people in normal residential housing with no purpose-built shelter.

Table 9 Percentage blast casualties

Zone	Dead	Injured	Uninjured by blast
A	98	2	0
B	50	40	10
C	5	45	50
D	0	25	75

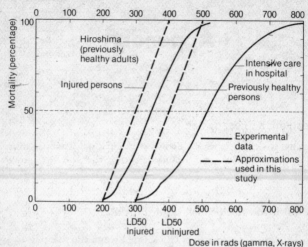

Fig. 21 Mortality in relation to radiation dose

Note: These mortality relationships apply for *acute* doses of radiation, that is a dose of radiation received over a day or two. Doses received over a longer period are called *chronic* and have fewer severe effects. The 50% mortality/lethal dose (the LD50 dose) is somewhat uncertain, but is expected to range from about 350 to 500 rads for healthy adults, depending on the extent of medical care available. The lower LD50 value of 350 rads (data from Hiroshima) is the most relevant for this study because people would be exposed to infections and because intensive hospital treatment such as bone-marrow transplants would not be available. In our study, radiation is received from fall-out, and while most of the total radiation is received within a day or so, an appreciable amount is received after this. We decided to take into account the fact that radiation does not cease after a day or so, by using the two-week accumulated dose in conjunction with an LD50 dose of 400 rads. This choice of LD50 can be justified because 77–87% of the two-week accumulated dose is received within two days, thus, even for borderline cases receiving just 400 rads in two weeks, an almost lethal to lethal acute dose of 310 to 350 rads is received in the first two days. On top of this, another 50 to 90 rads would be received over the next twelve days.

Application of our LD50 values to a typical population probably underestimates the numbers of deaths from radiation because:
● People continue to receive radiation long after the two-week period.
● A lower LD50 value should be used for children and the elderly who are much more susceptible to radiation.
● Our reduction of 100 rads in the LD50 for those injured is probably an underestimate; some sources suggest that a reduction of 200 rads or more would be more appropriate.[6]

In any case, the casualty figures we obtain are not very sensitive to even quite

Taking for example a case where 10,000 people were inside Zone B, 5,000 would be killed, 4,000 injured, and 1,000 uninjured by blast. In some cases there can be complications in the counting procedure when bombs are assumed to explode near enough to each other for the blast rings to overlap. In this case it was assumed in our calculations that one bomb exploded first. One set of casualties was calculated first, and for the second bomb, additional casualties were worked out using the now smaller population left after the first bomb. This gives a very conservative estimate of the total because those already injured by the first bomb are much more likely to be killed by the second. This is particularly true in Zones B and C where blast damage would have destroyed most protection from the heat of the fire-ball and many fatal burns would be received.

Assumptions relating to the London study

Population figures were based on the GLC 1977 census and counted on a borough basis. A uniform population density was assumed in residential areas inside each borough. Areas of open land, parks, airfields, rivers, etc. were assumed to have no resident population. If a surprise attack were to occur on a working day in London the census figures would be much too low and casualty figures would be many times higher because of the large numbers of people who commute into the capital during the day. Also, in summer the population is substantially increased by visitors.

Burns casualties

The numbers of people affected by burns are impossible to work out accurately because of the very wide variation depending on conditions. The most important factor is the number of people in the open or near windows. Sheltering inside away from windows will give protection against the intense heat of the fire-ball because the heat is dissipated before the blast wave arrives. Subsequent

---

a large change in LD50 value. For example, our casualty figures for the higher PF and an LD50 value of 400 rads, can equally be interpreted as those applying for a lower PF, but with an unrealistically high LD50 of 800 rads. For our study, this results in only a 16% reduction in deaths.

Data are taken from the National Radiological Protection Board, NRPB – R87, 1979, pp. 43–4.

bombs would cause far more burns casualties because badly damaged housing in Zones B and C would give little protection. Weather conditions are also quite important. Snow on the ground or a cloud base above the fire-ball reflects heat very efficiently and extends the fire and burns zones. The general visibility is also important, although even if the weather is hazy, burns would still be received a long way from the explosion. More important in hazy weather is that heat is reflected in all directions and burns could be received *even out of the line of sight of the fire-ball.*

Radiation casualties

As in the blast calculation, casualties are worked out by adding up the number of people in particular zones. In this case the zones are defined by particular radiation contours corresponding to doses accumulated over two weeks.

As mentioned in Chapter 2 the likelihood of dying from a given dose of radiation rises very sharply in the 300–500 rad range. Figure 21 shows mortality/dose graphs and limits used to calculate the number of people killed by radiation from fall-out. The mortality graphs are not completely straight in reality but curve over at the top and bottom ends. Using straight lines, however, is a good approximation and makes calculations much easier. Our procedure allows for the fact that injured people are much more vulnerable to radiation – for these people a dose of 300 rads is considered sufficient to kill half of them.

For areas *not* affected by blast, it is assumed that there are no injured and a zone defined by received doses of 300 and 500 rads is used in which 43 per cent of the people are killed.

For areas affected by blast levels above 1 p.s.i. (all of London) there *are* injured people, and the radiation zone is defined by doses above 200 and below 500 rads. Below 200 rads we count no deaths and above 500 everyone is killed. Most people fall into one of these two categories. A relatively small number fall into the 200–500 rads-received zones within each blast zone (the 'borderline' area shown in Figure 22). For each blast zone there are differing numbers of injured people and as a result radiation will kill different proportions of those surviving. The proportions used in this study are shown in Table 10.

To calculate the final death and injury totals the dose received in a given area has to be worked out. In any area the dose received is given by the radiation received in the open, divided by the

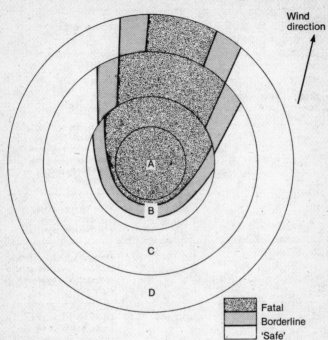

Wind direction

Fatal

Borderline

'Safe'

Fig. 22 Radiation zones

Table 10 Percentage casualties due to the combined effects of blast and radiation in the dose range 200–500 rads for different blast zones

Zone	Dead	Injured	Uninjured	Borderline radiation cases
A	100	0	0	0
B	59	18	8	15
C	16	20	38	26
D	6	11	57	26

Table 11 Protection factors and radiation contours for casualty calculation

Blast Zone	Lower PF Limit	Upper PF limit	Radiation contours needed for casualty calculation (200 and 500 rads × PF values)	Comments
A	1	1	200, 400	In this zone housing is completely destroyed and gives no protection. 400 is the upper value because there are no people uninjured
B	1		200, 500	Housing is destroyed or very badly damaged and can give little protection
		2	400, 1,000	
C	2		400, 1,000	Damaged partitions, doors, roofs, and windows admit radiation but give limited protection
		5	1,000, 2,500	
D	5		1,000, 2,500	Lower value takes into account blast damage to roofs and windows
		10	2,000, 5,000	Upper value of 10 is a HO value for an *undamaged* house and is therefore not valid. This value was used only for purposes of comparison

protection factor (PF). (Appendix 3 describes how PF values are calculated.) In our calculations a range of PF values was considered in each blast-damage zone (see Table 11). Therefore for each blast zone different radiation contours need to be known, and these, after division by the PF value, give dose-received levels of 200 and 500 rads.

Zone B can now again be taken as an example of the calculation. If there were 10,000 people inside Zone B, blast would kill 5,000, injure 4,000 and leave 1,000 unhurt. Once radiation is taken into account the picture changes very dramatically. It is simplest to look at three smaller zones inside Zone B (Figure 22) showing 'fatal', 'borderline', and 'safe' areas.

In the diagram the populations of these zones are: 5,000 in the 'fatal' area; 1,000 in the 'borderline' area; and 4,000 in the 'safe' area.

In Zone B/fatal, all of the 5,000 people die as a result of the one-megaton bomb; 2,500 would be killed by blast, and 2,500 by radiation over the next few weeks.

In Zone B/borderline, 500 people would be killed by the blast and 90 more within a few weeks from radiation effects. Towards the outer edges of this zone there would be 260 people who would not die of radiation sickness, 180 of whom would be injured by the blast. A further 150 people would have doses of radiation just sufficient to kill them and could take months to die.

In Zone B/'safe' there would be 2,000 killed by blast, 1,600 injured, and 400 uninjured.

Adding up all these figures gives the final toll of casualties after a few months as: killed, 7,740 (77%); injured, 1,780 (18%); uninjured, 480 (5%).

Radiation leaves very few survivors in Zone B.

Appendix
5

The effects of a nuclear strike upon a nuclear reactor

Nuclear reactors or reprocessing plants would certainly be important targets in any nuclear war, however 'limited'. In the Square Leg exercise both the Dungeness B nuclear reactor and the Windscale nuclear waste-reprocessing plants were attacked by ground-burst nuclear weapons.

Such an attack has very serious consequences because in addition to the radiation produced by the ground-burst nuclear weapon, the highly radioactive nuclear fuel in the reactor core is vaporised and spread out over a wide area. The contents of the reactor core remain radioactive for a very long time so that high radiation levels persist much longer than from a nuclear bomb alone (see Figure 24). Vast areas of land could be made uninhabitable, by peacetime radiation standards, by just *one* bomb on a nuclear reactor. Even at a dose of 2 rads per year (four times the currently acceptable peacetime level for a member of the public) 1,200 square miles of land would remain unfit for human use for a year after the attack, representing 1 per cent of the entire land area of the UK.

Just ten bombs targeted on ten nuclear power stations around the periphery of the country would have a devastating effect no matter what the wind direction. People over large areas of the country could be at risk from potentially lethal levels of radiation. So far we have only considered reactors in the UK, but in any credible attack, reactors in other European countries would also be targets. The UK

Nuclear power stations and laboratories in the U.K.

1 Hinkley Point	7 Dungeness	13 Hartlepool
2 Oldbury	8 Bradwell	14 Wylfa
3 Berkeley	9 Sizewell	15 Heysham
4 Harwell	10 Trawsfynydd	16 Chapelcross
5 Aldermaston	11 Calder Hall	17 Hunterston
6 Winfrith	12 Windscale	18 Dounreay

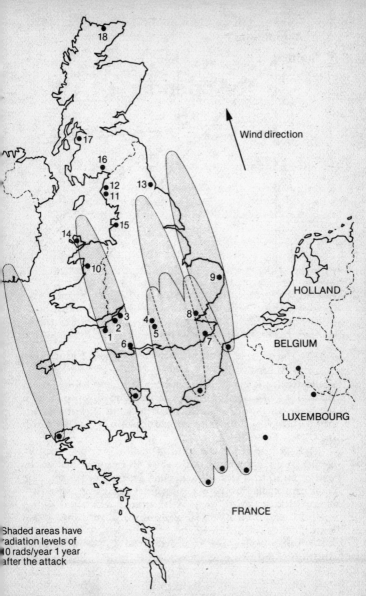

Wind direction

HOLLAND

BELGIUM

LUXEMBOURG

FRANCE

Shaded areas have
radiation levels of
0 rads/year 1 year
after the attack

Fig. 23 Fall-out from nuclear reactors in Europe

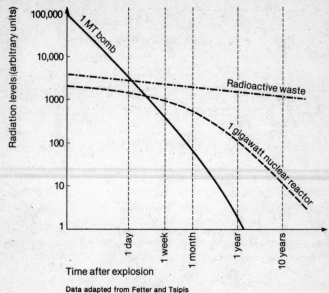

Fig. 24 The decay of fall-out radiation from a ground-burst on open country, on a nuclear reactor, and on radioactive waste

would receive fall-out from many of the explosions in France, Holland, or Germany, depending on the wind direction. With a southerly wind, as in Square Leg, fall-out from nuclear weapons striking French nuclear reactors would be blown over a large area of the UK (see Figure 23).

Certainly, vaporising the cores of nuclear reactors is a very efficient way of desolating large areas of a country. Indeed, by waiting for suitable weather conditions, a determined or desperate combatant could devastate a substantial part of an opponent's industrial capacity with a single weapon: so could a terrorist group equipped with a small nuclear weapon or a small nation with a limited number of nuclear weapons.

For further reading see S. A. Fetter and K. Tsipis, *Scientific American*, April 1981, p.33.

Appendix
6

The nuclear arsenal

Nuclear weapons can be divided into three main categories:

- Strategic weapons
- Eurostrategic weapons (or theatre weapons)
- Tactical weapons

Strategic Nuclear Weapons

These are long-range weapons designed primarily for an inter-continental nuclear exchange. They are maintained in large numbers by both the USA and the USSR and to a lesser extent by the UK, France, and China. Strategic nuclear warheads can be delivered to their targets either by missiles or by long-range bombers.

Table 12 shows the main type of strategic weapons held by the two superpowers in 1981. These weapons include Intercontinental Ballistic Missiles (ICBMs) which are launched from underground silos, Submarine-Launched Ballistic Missiles (SLBMs), aircraft-carried nuclear bombs, and aircraft-carried Short-Range Nuclear Attack Missiles (SRAMs). In general the Soviet weapons are somewhat less accurate than the American ones, but the Soviet missiles have larger warheads (more explosive power) to make up for this. Some ballistic missiles carry more than one warhead. Such missiles are termed MIRVed because they contain Multiple Independently targetable Re-entry Vehicles, i.e. one missile con-tains several nuclear warheads which can be independently targeted on re-entry into the Earth's atmosphere after an inter-continental flight through space.

The range of the Soviet and American ICBMs varies between 4,500 and 8,000 miles, and the range of SLBMs between 1,500 and 4,500 miles. The range limitation of SLBMs is due to the limited size of missile that can be accommodated on board a submarine. SLBMs must therefore be launched from positions closer to their targets

Table 12 Strategic weapons of the superpowers 1981

Vehicle	Number deployed	Independently targetable warheads per missile	Total yield per missile (MT)	Accuracy* (metres)
USA				
ICBMs:				
Minuteman II	450	1	1.5	400
Minuteman III	550	3	0.51	300
Minuteman III	100	3	1.05	300
Titan II	52	1	10	1,300
SLBMs:				
Polaris A–3	80	3	0.6	900
Poseidon C–3	320	10	0.4	500
Trident C–4	200	8	0.8	500
Bombers:		Nuclear weapons per aircraft		
B–52	348	4–12	about 0.5	180

USSR		Nuclear weapons per aircraft		
ICBMs:				
SS-11	460	1	1 or 0.6	1,000–1,800
SS-13	60	1	1	1,300
SS-17	150	4	2	300–600
SS-18	240	8	4	300–600
SS-18	60	1	15	1,000–2,500
SS-19	360	6	3	300–450
SLBMs:				
SS-N-6	438	1 or 2	1 or 0.4	1,400
SS-N-8	290	1	1	1,000–1,500
SS-NX-17	12	1	1	500
SS-N-18	192	3	0.6	500–1,000
Bombers:				
Mya-4 'Bison'	56	1	..	..
Tu-95 'Bear'	100	2	..	..

*Circular Error Probable (CEP), i.e. radius of a circle around a target within which a weapon aimed at that target has a 50% probability of falling.

Data from Stockholm International Peace Research Institute[55]

Table 13 Primary eurostrategic weapons 1979

Missiles

	Weapon	Number deployed	Independently targetable warheads per missile	Total yield per missile (MT)	Accuracy (metres)
USSR	SS-4*	390	1	1	2,400
	SS-5*	80	1	1	1,250
	SS-12*	72	1	1	?
	SS-20*	120	3	0.15	400
	SS-N-5†	18	1	1–2	?
USA	Pershing IA	180	1	0.06–0.4	450
UK	Polaris A–3†	64	1	0.6	800
France	S–2†	18	1	0.15	?
	M–20†	64	1	1	?

Note: In 1983 NATO plans to introduce Pershing II missiles and Ground-Launched Cruise Missiles (GLCMs) in Europe.

Aircraft	Type	Number deployed	Nuclear weapons per aircraft	Speed (mach no.)
USSR	Tu–16 Badger	318	2	0.8
	Tu–22M Backfire	60	4	2.5
USA	FB–111A‡	66	6	2.5
	F–111E/F	156	2	2.2/2.5
UK	Vulcan B2	48	2	0.95
France	Mirage IVA	33	1	2.2

* IRBMs
† SLBMs
‡ Not based in Europe but intended for use in Europe
Note: Mach 1 = the speed of sound, or approximately 760 m.p.h.
Data from Stockholm International Peace Research Institute[55]

than ICBMs. Recent advances in methods of submarine detection and anti-submarine warfare have resulted in the Americans developing the very large Trident submarines, whose missiles have longer ranges. Trident submarines can therefore operate at a safer distance from the enemy.

The Air-Launched Cruise Missile (ALCM) developed by the USA can be fired from B-52 bombers. The USAF plans to deploy 3,400 of these in 1983. These missiles have a range of over 2,000 miles and fly at a subsonic speed at low altitudes to avoid radar detection. They carry sophisticated optical sensors and computers with memorised ground-contour maps so that they can navigate extremely accurately and thereby fly zig-zag courses to explode within tens of metres of their designated targets. The Americans are also currently considering the possible deployment of the MX ICBMs in the next few years. The MX missiles will have much higher accuracy than present-day ICBMs and were originally intended to be shunted around a large subterranean network of tunnels between silos so that their precise location would not be known. At present it seems likely that these missiles will be sited in existing Minuteman silos.

The total explosive power of the combined American and Soviet strategic nuclear forces is now about 8,000 MT.

Eurostrategic weapons

These are intermediate-range nuclear weapons deployed in or intended for use within Europe; they are sometimes called 'theatre' nuclear weapons. They are able to penetrate well inside enemy territory. Eurostrategic weapons are deployed by NATO, by France (a member of NATO though with independent military command), and by the Warsaw Pact. Table 13 lists the primary Eurostrategic weapons located in Europe. These weapons include Intermediate-Range Ballistic Missiles (IRBMs), SLBMs, and supersonic aircraft capable of delivering nuclear bombs and SRAMs. The ranges of these weapons vary between about 500 and 2,500 miles.

NATO plans to introduce 108 Pershing II IRBMs and 464 Ground-Launched Cruise Missiles (GLCMs) in 1983 as part of its 'modernisation' programme. Pershing II missiles employ a sophisticated guidance system incorporating a video radar which scans the target area and enables them to hit their targets with an accuracy of about 45 metres. These missiles would be able to travel well inside the Soviet Union within a few minutes of launch. The

GLCMs, launched from mobile transporters, are also highly accurate (30–90 metres) but they fly close to the ground at subsonic speeds like ALCMs. GLCMs could be detected easily only by airborne early-warning radar systems. The British Government has accepted in principle the deployment of 160 GLCMs in the UK at Molesworth, near Huntingdon, and at Greenham Common, near Newbury. It should be noted, however, that these new weapons will be under US control and could be launched without the intervention of the host country – a matter of some concern. The USSR is currently deploying SS-20 IRBMs with an estimated accuracy of 400 metres and a range of 2,500 miles. There were about 180 deployed in Eastern Europe at the end of 1980. Indeed, 'the new Eurostrategic weapons on both sides of the NATO/WTO [Warsaw Treaty Organisation] border must be seen as an enhancement of war-fighting capabilities. The enhanced effectiveness of the new weapons makes all of Europe more vulnerable to nuclear devastation.'[55]

Tactical nuclear weapons

Tactical weapons are short-range nuclear weapons (about 15 miles) intended for use on the battlefield. They include nuclear shells fired by artillery, low-yield nuclear bombs, and enhanced radiation weapons (neutron bombs) designed primarily for use against tanks. Although these weapons are of low yield (a few kilotons) when compared with strategic weapons, they are nevertheless 'nuclear' devices in the true sense and cause intense blast, heat, and radiation, and contaminate the surrounding countryside and civilian areas with radioactive fall-out. Before 1977 it was estimated that over one-third of the 1,600 US-built artillery pieces in Europe, including 155 mm field guns and 8-inch Howitzers, were capable of firing either conventional or nuclear shells.[56] Since then a programme of modernisation has provided many more artillery batteries with this dual capacity and the Americans are going ahead with production of 155 mm nuclear shells for use in Europe. Plans to introduce neutron warheads for the 8-inch Howitzers have met with some European opposition, although the Americans are stockpiling them for possible deployment should they be required. Neutron bombs are designed to produce a much larger flux of high-energy neutrons than normal nuclear bombs, releasing about 80 per cent of their energy in this form. These fast neutrons emitted during the explosion give a high radiation dose to troops and tank crews which will make them extremely ill and then kill them within a few days. These weapons are controversial because they can kill people at a range of several miles without actually damaging property at that distance because the effects of heat and blast are less significant. The Warsaw Pact also has nuclear-capable artillery and short-range nuclear missiles called 'FROG'. The numbers of these are uncertain.

Notes

References to publications quoted or referred to more than once are given thus: 6/24. The numbers are page references, the first to this book, the second to the publication in question (except that Home Office internal circulars are referred to by section rather than page). No page number is given when a publication is referred to as a whole.

1. *Defence – outline of future policy*, HMSO, 1957, Cmnd 124.
2. S. Zuckerman, *Nuclear Illusion and Reality*, Collins, 1982, p. 51.
3. A. W. Oughterson and S. Warren (eds.), *Medical Effects of the Atomic Bomb in Japan*, McGraw-Hill, 1956.
   (see also: National Research Council of Japan, Special Committee for the Investigation of the Effects of the Atomic Bomb, *Medical Report on Atomic Bomb Effects*, 1953.)
4. Office of Technology Assessment (Congress of the United States), *The Effects of Nuclear War*, Croom Helm, 1980: 71/8.
5. US Department of Defense and US Department of Energy (S. Glasstone and P. J. Dolan eds.), *The Effects of Nuclear Weapons*, Castle House, 1980: 24/522–3; 74/442.
6. Stockholm International Peace Research Institute (J. Rotblat), *Nuclear Radiation in Warfare*, Taylor and Francis, 1981: 19/34; 76/40, 114/36.
7. P. J. Lindop, 'Radiation Aspects of Nuclear War in Europe' (Conference on Nuclear War in Europe), Groningen, 1981: 21/91; 53/94.
8. T. Akizuki, *Nagasaki 1945*, Quartet, 1981, pp. 118, 122.
9. D. Moralee, 'EMP – the forgotten threat?', *Electronics and Power*, July/August 1981.
10. D. Campbell, 'World War III – an exclusive preview', *New Statesman*, 3 October 1980. (see also: 'Scotland's nuclear targets', *New Statesman*, 6 March 1981.)
11. *Domestic Nuclear Shelters: Technical Guidance*, HMSO, 1981: 26/2; 44/18, 83, 85; 46/18, 105; 108/41; 110/18.
12. Hansard, written answers to questions, 203, defence, 6 March 1981.

13. London Borough of Islington War Emergency Plan.

14. *Protect and Survive*, HMSO, 1980: 30/3, 7; 32/7; 52/24; 56/24; 91/3, 7.

15. Home Office, Circular ES1/1979, 'Food and Agriculture Controls in War', section 12.

16. Watford District War Emergency Plan: 34/Pt2 VII, Pt1 X.

17. D. Smith, *The Defence of the Realm in the 80's*, Croom Helm, 1980: 95/89–102.

18. Home Office, Circular ES1/1981, 'Civil Defence Review': 35/2; 85/3.

19. Hansard, Home Secretary's announcement to Parliament, 7 August 1980.

20. Home Office, Circular ES5/1974, 'War Emergency Planning for the Fire Service', section 4.

21. *Greater London Housing Condition Survey*, 1981, p. 162.

22. Home Office, Circular ES6/1976, 'Water Services in War': 57/5; 59/5; 60/6.

23. *Nuclear Weapons*, HMSO, 1981: 62/3; 108/55.

24. Home Office, Circular ES3/1976, 'Briefing Material for Wartime Controllers': 64/11; 68/13, 4; 69/6; 70/10.

25. A. Haines, 'Possible Consequences of a Nuclear Attack on London', paper read to the Medical Campaign Against Nuclear Weapons, London, January 1981.

26. Department of Health and Social Security, HDC(1977)1, 'The Preparation and Organization of the Health Service for War', p. 9, section 62.

27. J. Karas and J. Stanbury, 'Fatal radiation syndrome from an accidental nuclear explosion', *New England Journal of Medicine*, Vol. 272, 1965, p. 755.

28. K. D. Steidley, G. S. Zeit, and R. Ouellette, 'Another ^{60}Co hot cell accident', *Health Physics*, Vol. 36, 1979, p. 437.

29. J. Smith and A. Smith, 'Attitudes towards civil defence and psychological effects of nuclear war', *British Medical Journal*, Vol. 283, 1981, p. 963.

30. A. Gellhorn and P. Janeway, 'Nuclear disaster: the medical response', proceedings of the First Congress of International Physicians for the Prevention of Nuclear War, Airlie House, Virginia, USA, March 1981.

31. Home Office, Circular ES8/1976, 'Environmental Health in War': 67/9, 4.

32. Central Electricity Generating Board, *Statistical Year-Book 1977/78.*

33. 'Revealed: the elite 'phone list for disaster day', *Time Out*, 23–29 January 1981.

34. P. Rodgers, M. Dando, P. van den Dungen, *As Lambs to the Slaughter*, Arrow, 1981, p. 175.

35. K. R. Lassey, 'Transfer of radiostrontium and radiocaesium from soil to diet – models consistent with fall-out analyses', *Health Physics*, Vol. 37, 1979, p. 557.

36. I. Ishikawa and D. L. Swain (translators), *Hiroshima and Nagasaki – the physical, medical, and social effects of the atomic bombings*, Hutchinson, 1981.

37. J. L. Lyon and others, 'Childhood leukaemia associated with fall-out from nuclear testing', *New England Journal of Medicine*, Vol. 300, 1979, p. 397.

38. International Commission on Radiological Protection Recommendations (ICRP), No. 26, Pergamon Press, 1977.

39. J. Hampson, 'Photochemical war on the atmosphere', *Nature*, Vol. 250, 1974, p. 189. P. Goldsmith and others: 'Nitrogen oxides, nuclear weapon testing, Concorde, and stratospheric ozone', *Nature*, Vol. 244, 1973, p. 545.

40. G.C. Reinsel, 'Analysis of total ozone data for the detection of recent trends and the effects of nuclear testing during the 1960's', *Geophysical Research Letters*, Vol. 8, 1981, p. 1227.

41. A. J. P. Taylor, *English History 1914–45*, Oxford University Press, 1965, p. 502.

42. P. Laurie, *Beneath the City Streets*, Granada, 1979: 82/120; 83/178–246.

43. Home Office, Circular ES7/1973, 'Machinery of Government in War': *Planning Assumptions and General Guidance*: 83/6, 4; 84/5.

44. D. Campbell, in *New Statesman*, 19 September 1980.

45. Home Office, Circular ES3/1973, 'Home Defence Planning Assumptions', section 1.

46. L. Godfrey, 'Seminar for Survival', *Protect and Survive Monthly*, May 1981.

47. S. Openshaw and P. Steadman, 'On the Geography of a Worst Case Nuclear Attack on the Population of Britain' in a forthcoming *Political Geography Quarterly*.

48. *Sanity*, February/March 1981, p. 2.

49. 'The Strangelove HQ under MAD mountain', *Observer*, 7 September 1980.

50. Stockholm International Peace Research Institute, 'World Armaments and Disarmament', *SIPRI Yearbook 1981*, Taylor and Francis, 1981, pp. 21, 275.

51. US House of Representatives Committee on Foreign Affairs, *The modernization of NATO's long-range theater nuclear forces*, US Government Printing Office, Washington, 1981: 94/vii; 95/12.

52. Hansard, House of Lords, 843, 23 April 1980.

53. 'Louis Mountbatten 1979/80: A military commander surveys the nuclear arms race', *International Security*, Vol. 4 (No. 3), pp. 3–5.

54. Press Conference, 6 May 1977, reprinted in *Survival*, July/August 1977.

55. Stockholm International Peace Research Institute: 'World Armaments and Disarmament', *SIPRI Yearbooks 1980* and *1981*, Taylor and Francis, 1980, 1981.

56. 'NATO increases short-range nuclear arms', *Guardian*, 28 October 1981.

Further Reading

Home Office publications

Protect and Survive, HMSO, 1980
Domestic Nuclear Shelters, HMSO, 1981
Domestic Nuclear Shelters: Technical Guidance, HMSO, 1981
Nuclear Weapons, HMSO, 1981
Civil Defence – why we need it, HMSO, 1981

Effects of nuclear weapons

Three very comprehensive reference works are:
The Effects of Nuclear Weapons, US Department of Defence and
   Department of Energy, J. Glasstone and P. J. Dolan (eds.), Castle
   House, 1980
The Effects of Nuclear War, Office of Technology Assessment
   (Congress of the United States), Croom Helm, London, 1980
Nuclear Radiation in Warfare, J. Rotblat, Taylor and Francis,
   London, 1981

Information on weapons systems and numbers of weapons

Stockholm International Peace Research Insitute (SIPRI), various
   yearbooks
The Military Balance, International Institute of Strategic Studies
   (IISS), London, 1980
A Comprehensive Study of Nuclear Weapons, United Nations
   special report, New York, 1980

Wider issues

Nuclear Illusion and Reality, S. Zuckerman, Collins, London, 1982
How to make your mind up about the bomb, R. Neild, Andre
   Deutsch, London, 1981
The defence of the realm in the 1980s, Dan Smith, Croom Helm,
   London, 1980
The Third World War: August 1985, General Sir John Hackett and
   others, Sidgwick and Jackson, London, 1978
As Lambs to the Slaughter, P. Rogers, M. Dando, P. van den
   Dungen, Arrow, London, 1981

Organisations

Architects for Peace, 41 St James Road, Sevenoaks, Kent

Campaign for Nuclear Disarmament (CND), 11 Goodwin Street, London N4

Campaign for Survival (Ecoropa), PO Box 11, Godalming, Surrey

European Nuclear Disarmament (END), 277 Seven Sisters Road, London N7

Friends of the Earth (FOE), 9 Poland Street, London W11

Greenpeace, 36 Graham Street, London N1

Journalists Against Nuclear Extermination (JANE), c/o Magazine Branch, Acorn House, 314 Grays Inn Road, London WC1

Medical Association for the Prevention of War (MAPW), 576 Somerton Road, London NW2

Medical Campaign Against Nuclear Weapons (MCANW), 23a Tenison Road, Cambridge

Nursing Campaign Against Nuclear Weapons (NCANW), 11 Charlotte Street, Bristol 1

Russell Peace Foundation, Bertrand Russell House, Gamble Street, Nottingham

Scientists Against Nuclear Arms (SANA), 11 Chapel Street, Woburn Sands, Milton Keynes

United Nations Association, 3 Whitehall Court, London SW1

World Disarmament Campaign (WDC), 21 Little Russell Street, London WC1

Index